Jane Feather

The last of the prophets

A study of the life, teaching and character of John the Baptist

Jane Feather

The last of the prophets
A study of the life, teaching and character of John the Baptist

ISBN/EAN: 9783337112868

Printed in Europe, USA, Canada, Australia, Japan

Cover: Foto ©Lupo / pixelio.de

More available books at **www.hansebooks.com**

HANDBOOKS

FOR

BIBLE CLASSES

AND PRIVATE STUDENTS

EDITED BY

PROFESSOR MARCUS DODS, D.D.

AND

REV. ALEXANDER WHYTE, D.D.

THE LAST OF THE PROPHETS—JOHN THE BAPTIST
BY REV. J. FEATHER

EDINBURGH
T. & T. CLARK, 38 GEORGE STREET
1894

THE LAST OF THE PROPHETS

*A STUDY OF
THE LIFE, TEACHING, AND CHARACTER
OF
JOHN THE BAPTIST*

BY

REV. J. FEATHER

EDINBURGH
T. & T. CLARK, 38 GEORGE STREET

PREFACE

WHILE the rest of the great characters of Scripture have had much study bestowed on them, and deservedly so, standing as they did at the turning-points of national history, or holding aloft the word of life in dark and cloudy days, John the Baptist, who closes the Old Dispensation and inaugurates the New, has seemed to suffer a strange neglect. The books upon his life and character are few, even now. Yet his calm strength and nobleness, like that of a mountain, which does not shrink as the storm gathers about it and bursts upon it, the gloom of his environment, and the pathos of his end, make a picture without a parallel, even among the noble army of martyrs.

There are two reasons to account for this apparent neglect. First, his proximity to the greatest world-character of all, to whom he gave testimony, and in the presence of whom he bowed himself. John and Jesus—to resume our figure—are peaks in the same historic mountain-range; and all eyes, as is natural, are drawn to the higher, and all feet which have trod this Sinai at all, have endeavoured, in thought at least, to reach its highest slopes. In the radiance of the dayspring from on high, all earth-born fires, however large and bright, are paled. But if we set the gauge of our intention to John, we shall find him well worth our climbing, find "moral bracing in the breathing of his difficult air"; while, as we bring contemporaneous facts to his light, we shall see that they yield their meaning and significance.

The second reason is, the meagreness of the records. A few

brief notices in the New Testament, and a few well-known passages of Josephus, afford almost all we know of the external conditions of his life. It has been my endeavour in the following pages to expound the bearing and draw out the treasures of these. But, going behind them, I have tried to reach the springs of his character, and to exhibit the relations he held to the world of his own day. However it may have succeeded, there is here the attempt made to answer those requirements which Carlyle lays down for true biography: "How did the world and man's life, from his particular position, represent themselves to his mind? How did co-existing circumstances modify him from without; how did he modify these from within? With what endeavours and what efficacy rule over them; with what resistance and what suffering sink under them?"

In the course of this "study," I have freely used the various "Lives of Christ," and available authorities on the different subjects as they have arisen. To them I am under much obligation, and where they are quoted, I trust they are acknowledged.[1] Fortunately, the life of the Baptist does not afford, with one or two exceptions, a theological battle-ground. It and its import are rather matters for clear apprehension than for citation of authorities. And as the character is of much more consequence than the controversy, I have refrained from introducing the latter, except where it seemed needful for the removal of obstacles to apprehension of the former. I would offer this book as a contribution to the better understanding of one of the purest and loftiest lives which have ever blessed the world, and shall be glad if it accomplishes, in any appreciable degree, that end.

J. F.

CROYDON, *August* 1894.

[1] More than a word of general acknowledgment is due to the exhaustive and scholarly work of Dr. Reynolds on "John the Baptist." It is a careful, candid, and able piece of work.

	PAGE
INTRODUCTION	11
CHAP. I.—HOME LIFE	21
CHAP. II.—"IN THE DESERTS"	32
CHAP. III.—"THE THOUGHT THAT BREATHES" . . .	43
CHAP. IV.—"THE WORD THAT BURNS"	53
CHAP. V.—"THE WRATH TO COME"	61
CHAP. VI.—"WHAT THEN MUST *WE* DO?" . . .	71
CHAP. VII.—"THE BAPTISM OF JOHN" . . .	79
CHAP. VIII.—"COMEST *THOU* TO *ME*?" . . .	88
CHAP. IX.—"I SAW AND BARE RECORD"	103
(α) TO THE DEPUTATION	104
(β) TO HIS OWN DISCIPLES	108
(γ) THE "SON OF GOD"	111
(δ) THE BRIDEGROOM	119
CHAP. X.—ON THE STEEP SLOPE	122
CHAP. XI.—OVER THE PRECIPICE	134
CHAP. XII.—JESUS ; AND NEMESIS	139
NOTE A—ST. LUKE I. 5—II. 52	147
NOTE B—"SON OF GOD"	153

THE LAST OF THE PROPHETS

INTRODUCTION

By the time at which the New Testament opens, the Mediterranean Sea had become a Roman lake. For a couple of centuries Rome had been steadily advancing her boundaries, subduing and making tributary the nations, even the strongest, which opposed her in her fate-like march to universal conquest; until, at the death of Augustus (A.D. 14), all the countries which sloped towards the Great Sea acknowledged her authority. Cæsar's writ ran in all the lands from the Atlantic seaboard on the west to the Armenian mountains, the river Tigris, and the Arabian deserts on the east; from the Great Desert of Africa and the cataracts of the Nile, up to the Caucasian range of mountains, the Black Sea, the Danube, and the Rhine, beyond which lay the impregnable forests and fierce tribes of Germany, to the English Channel on the north. Only the barriers of nature itself seemed strong enough to stop the march of this imperial race. A glance at the map shows that she ruled over all we are accustomed to regard as the civilised world. Sometimes by direct conquest; sometimes by taking advantage of the straitened circumstances of other peoples, proclaiming a protectorate, then absorbing those whom it protected, this world-empire had been built up, until there was no place, and it stood alone in the midst of the earth.

To become the vassals of this conquering people was, to the

Jews, to enter upon the last act of a long and gloomy tragedy. Medo-Persian, Greek, Egyptian, and Græco-Syrian in turn had ruled over the proud and restless race which inhabited a country about the size of the principality of Wales. Unfortunately it lay in the line of march between the growing Western and the waning Eastern powers; and behind them all we catch glimpses now and again of the Roman in his steady, calm oncoming, who cleared them all out of his path and spread his authority over the land as he advanced.

From the death of Alexander the Great (B.C. 323), under whom they had been at peace, there had come a long succession of dark and cloudy days for the ill-starred Jews. Oppressions, unbearable in their weight and sickening in their cruelty, bore them down and broke their spirit. Between the Ptolemies and Seleucidæ they were frequently between the upper and nether millstones. In the times of comparative quiet which followed upon their acceptance of the first Ptolemy, the people grew and multiplied, alike in numbers and in wealth. And again Jeshurun, having waxed fat, began to kick. Greek manners and morals began to insinuate themselves into Hebrew society, bringing in their wake that dry-rot among the foundations, which, in the nature of things, is ever the result of moral laxity. Additional to this, in the case of the Jews, was the fact that this development invaded and weakened the belief which was their very *raison d'être* as a race,—their separateness to Jehovah as the people for His own possession,—a belief they had cherished, defined more clearly and held more closely as persecutions and captivity had repeatedly borne down on them from outside nations; while at the same time it militated against the sacredness of their high ideal, sapping the strength of the confidence that Jehovah would be mindful of His own and deliver them.

The Hellenising party grew to be the party of power. It strengthened itself greatly during the earlier years of the reign of Antiochus Epiphanes (B.C. 175-164), to whom the province passed, with the sanction of Rome, on the defeat of Egypt. Joshua obtained by bribe the high priesthood, and changed his name to Jason. He built a gymnasium, to which he attracted the youth of the city; he weaned them by degrees from the habits and opinions of their fathers, and trained them in a complete system of Grecian education, and allowed the services of the Temple to fall into disuse.[1] His successor, Menelaus, carried out the policy still further, intensifying it both by sacrilege and murder.

But action and reaction are opposite, if, in the moral sphere, they are not seen at once to be equal. Always had there been a party zealous for the law; and the widespreading, all-invading laxity of the period defined and focussed them, sharply outlining them against the dark background. The law—a law at once human and divine—which in our own history gave rise to Puritans and afterward to Methodists, produced in the age under consideration the *Chasidim*, or Pious, who, whatever they became by the New Testament period, at least originated in purity of motive. They stood to uphold the authority of the law, and to preserve the high theocratic ideal of national life and privilege.

The Jews had gained nothing and lost much in external condition by the substitution of the Syrian for the Egyptian dynasty. Especially under Antiochus Epiphanes did they find themselves beneath the harrow. When on an expedition to Egypt, a false rumour of his death gave rise to a religious insurrection against Menelaus the high priest, one of his creatures. "The intelligence of the insurrection, magnified into a deliberate revolt of the whole nation, reached Antiochus." He marched on Jerusalem, easily captured it, massacred many of its inhabitants, and desecrated with the most odious defilements the Temple and its sacred place, which the Jews had considered for centuries the one holy spot in the universe. But even this was not the end, as it was not the worst of his oppressions: we read of unresisting multitudes butchered in cold blood, of the inhibition of the national religion, the forcible substitution of idolatry, of sacrifices of swine, and of the most revolting cruelties upon those who were

[1] Milman.

faithful enough to disobey. Well might the Jews consider this period as forming one of the darkest and most fearful chapters in their history.

Again does the law of action and reaction enter. The *Chasidim* in religion become paralleled by the Maccabees in patriotism. The higher spirituality of life and devotion in the former looks across to a corresponding peak in the heroism of the latter. And the patriotism sprang out of the religion. A grand figure is that of old Mattathias, as, with his five sons behind him, he stands in the breach to dispute and defy the king's edict against the worship of Jehovah, and as he sinks, worn out with years and toil, in the midst of the fight : equally grand that of Judas, his son, who took the standard from the failing grasp of his dying father, rallied to it the zealous, the patriotic, the valorous of the people, carried it to victory after victory against veteran generals and disciplined troops who far outnumbered his own, until he seemed invincible ; and who, by his enterprise and sagacity, secured the results of his achievements and brought his country to the verge of becoming an independent state. If the former was one of the darkest, this is one of the brightest chapters in their national annals.

Yet it seems the very irony of fate that he, of all men, should be the means of bringing the power of Rome finally into the country for whose freedom he had fought. Knowing that he could not permanently maintain a conflict in which his enemies could bring into the field, and that continuously, thousands where he could only bring hundreds, that the sheer force of numbers must in the end prevail, he applied for an alliance with Rome, which was readily granted. But before the decree could reach him, his glorious career had ended. He was killed in battle, and died, as he had lived, the champion and hero of his country (B.C. 161).

Having once advanced her foot, Rome was not the power to withdraw it. She did not assume the sovereignty, nor was the alliance definitely maintained, but her claim was only held in abeyance, not abandoned ; and through all the long and intricate story which follows for a century, of civil war, and intrigue, and contending claims, she looms ever larger and nearer, until we find her, having conquered Syria, looking over the fair and fruitful land of Palestine. Not long was there need to wait for a pretext to enter it. Hyrcanus and Aristobulus were contending for the Jewish throne, and appealed to Pompey, who was lying at Damascus. He put them off for a while, but, becoming doubtful of the good faith of Aristobulus, and angry too that the Jews would not admit the arbitration of a foreigner, he laid siege to Jerusalem, which held out for three months. When it fell (B.C. 63), Pompey polluted with his presence the very Holy of Holies, but left the immense riches of the Temple intact. He nominated Hyrcanus ruler, and left. It was not the policy of the conquerors to enter at once on full possession of the conquered territory : Rome usually left a large autonomy to the people she subdued, on condition that her over-lordship was acknowledged and her tribute-money paid.

The Cæsars brought in the Herods, an Idumean dynasty, which, notwithstanding its benefits and magnificence, was never heartily accepted by the Jews. At this point Herod the Great comes upon the scene (B.C. 36). His almost superhuman vigour, his resolute will, his tact, his audacity, the greatness of his schemes, his lavish display and equally lavish gifts, gained for him his adjective. He *was* great in everything but personal character. But, as if he must carry the element of largeness into everything he did, he is distinguished among men by the enormity of his crimes. He was a very monster of iniquity. There is no need to re-tell at length his story : it is one of blood, while some of his freaks suggest insanity as the only explanation. The young and noble Aristobulus, who had the right to the priesthood ; his beautiful wife Mariamne, the only being, it is said, whom he really loved ; her mother ; his own three sons ; his uncle ; and some of his friends, all fell victims to his ambition, jealousy, or terror. He built theatres, introduced the looser Roman life into the midst of the people, and placed over the principal gate of

Jerusalem a golden eagle, the symbol of Imperial Rome. And thus, notwithstanding his gorgeous restoration of the Temple, he was hated by all who adhered to the national party. In all evil respects, Herod was a man to date from.

On his death, the ferment of the people began to manifest itself in uprisings and revolt, especially as the family dispute respecting his will made an interregnum. The garrison at Jerusalem at length found itself in the stress of great danger, and sent for help to Varus, the Roman general, then stationed at Antioch. When he had quelled the revolt, he took terrible revenge by the crucifixion of two thousand Jews. At length the emperor gave his decision on the will (A.D. 4), and "the rich and busy province of Galilee, with Perea, was assigned to Herod Antipas." [1]

As to the social condition of the country at this period, its withered state to-day, under the rule of "the unspeakable Turk," is in strange and humiliating contrast. "From early days the land of Canaan had been the scene of a busy, active life. . . . When the Hebrews entered it, they found a people already there in possession of the arts of life ; and they learned from them how to till the soil and grow the vine, the olive, and the fig. Vast flocks and herds roamed over the uplands, for they never gave up their pastoral occupations. . . . But they acquired by degrees a knowledge of all kinds of trades as well ; they opened mines for iron and copper ; with the help of the Phœnicians they learned the arts of building ; they were carpenters, smiths, and masons ; they made beautiful furniture, costly vessels, embroidered robes, fine jewels, musical instruments. . . . Galilee was famous for its corn, and on the lake the fishing trade was of great importance. . . . Flax was grown of different qualities, some coarse, some fine, and dried in the sun on the flat roofs of the houses, then it was made into ropes. The warm climate of Galilee enabled the indigo plant to be grown on the shores of the lake ; and Magdala, on the western coast, was well known for its dyeworks. The rich pastures of Samaria, as of the uplands east of the Jordan, were

---

[1] For the history, Josephus, The Apocrypha, Milman.

renowned for their breed of cattle. At Jericho the groves of palm were very valuable; and still more the gardens devoted to the balsam-shrub, precious both as a perfume and for medicinal properties. . . . Judea was not so well fitted for the growth of corn; but the fine turf of the downs near Hebron was thought to nurture specially fat lambs for sacrifice. Vine culture was general in the south; the steep slopes of the hillsides were cut into terraces carefully banked up with stones. . . . Many of the hills about Jerusalem were covered with valuable trees. Bethany, 'the house of dates,' was embowered in palms. Bethphage, 'the house of figs,' stood by a grove of fig-trees. . . . Jerusalem was not a manufacturing town; but a great variety of industries clustered round the Temple; and as the centre of the whole national life, not for the Jews of Palestine alone, but for those of the whole world, all kinds of commodities were brought to its markets." [1]

Although the state of religion in the nation, in its relation to John the Baptist and his to it, will form almost the gist and staple of the succeeding chapters, yet it is needful, to give something like completeness to our introductory sketch, that we should pass its salient features at the time of Herod Antipas under review, even if but briefly. It was at a very low ebb. The priesthood was largely a function, the high priesthood itself but a political office; while the puerilities of Scribes and Pharisees formed the spiritual aliment of the people,—much chaff and little grain.

To the Scribes was allotted the work and responsibility of making new copies of the sacred books,—the re-writing, in fact, of the nation's literature. After the return from the Captivity they became a recognised order, "rendered all the more necessary because at that time the Chaldee letters were adopted in place of the ancient Hebrew characters. Very naturally the transcriber and reader of Scripture became its expositor. By degrees, therefore, the Scribes assumed the office of public teachers; the very priests, unless also Scribes, taking a sub-

[1] Carpenter.

ordinate place. To their authority on doctrinal matters frequent appeal was made. As the oral as well as the written law was the subject of their teaching, they are constantly coupled with the Pharisees, the great exponents of the former. The scribe was the successor to the prophet. The prophet communicated new Scripture, the scribe guarded and elucidated the old."

The Pharisees formed the most powerful part of the nation. In their origin, far back in the sad days of "the mingling," they were, in some respects, the Methodists of their time, reducing conduct to order, to church observance, recognising the binding power of religion through the soul and all the activities of life down to the minutest details. "But the chief point of distinction lay in the regard paid by the Pharisees to the *oral* law, a series of unwritten interpretations of the divine oracles handed down from doctor to doctor, and forming an elaborate system extending to every detail of worship and of life. The 'traditions of the elders' thus spun around God's word a web of intricate refinement; and, while professing 'to fence the law,' or to lessen the risk of breaking it, became in the multiplicity of subtle distinctions and vexatious rules an oppression to the conscience. Formalism was substituted for spiritual religion, and the 'separateness' of this fraternity, as evinced by their long robes with fringe and tassels, their broad phylacteries, their long prayers publicly recited by the highways at the customary hours, as well as the casuistry of their teachings and the inconsistency of their lives, proved their piety to be in a great measure an affectation."

As for the Sadducees, they were the sceptics of their age, in the stricter and purer meaning of the word. The old party of the *Chasidim* (Pious) seems to have developed nuclei in the course of the years, and to have segregated into the Pharisees, Sadducees, and Essenes, according to the special formative principle of each cell, — obedience, morality, or self-control. "The Sadducees began with the supreme obligation of morality, and ended as mere rationalistic moralists; while from their rejection of the oral supplements to the Mosaic law, they proceeded to the denial of any doctrine not there plainly and literally taught, as that of a life after death. Possibly, also, their scepticism on this point was but an exaggeration of the view that God was not to be served *for the sake of* the reward of eternity,"—"that virtue was to be cultivated for its own sake, without calculation of consequences or hope of future recompense." They disallowed the oral interpretation of their great rivals the Pharisees. Their adherents were to be found chiefly among the upper classes, and they flattered themselves that the chief part of the intelligence and influence of the nation was included in their party. We can therefore readily see how such a position and belief would minister to a subtle self-flattery and a pride that pitied the rest of mankind.[1]

The position and beliefs these parties had come to hold by the time of John had grown up gradually through the centuries of prophetic silence; and seeing they claimed the sole interpretation of things divine, it is not to be greatly wondered at that when a prophet did arise, he should speedily find them in arms against him.

Through all these centuries, too, and through centuries before them, the Messianic hope had established and enlarged itself, until, by this period, it lay in the minds and hearts of the people and the sects alike (the Sadducees not excepted) extending its ramifications, like a root and its fibres, and ineradicable.

The very foundation of their national life and their separateness was religious. Divine truth and righteousness, and these as giving rise to a bright earthly hope, were their choicest heritage. Hence the high value the Hebrews had ever placed upon the prophets; who came, divinely commissioned, to re-affirm and re-enforce Jehovah's claims; to resuscitate and re-inspire the moral life of the people along the lines of the theocratic ideal. The prophets had been, in times past, the moral aristocracy of the nation; its divinely-given, divinely-inspired guides.

---

[1] Consult the section by Dr. Green on *Jewish Sects and Orders* in the Queen's Printers' Aids, where the subjects are well summarised, and from which some portions of the preceding three paragraphs are taken.

The paramount influence they had wielded, the high and sacred regard in which they were ever held, was due to their companionship with God. Jehovah had "uncovered their ears," talked with them, and from His presence they had come charged with the authoritative message. "Not by man, nor of the will of man" did they hold their office and exercise their function, but from Jehovah. They spoke with an authority greater than that of kings, for they belonged to a higher order. More than once had monarchs trembled at their rebukes and submissively done their bidding.

It was they who had written as with the finger of God, or spoken, with "thus saith Jehovah" as an introduction, those laws upon which their national life was based, and in the observance of which the divine benediction was found; they who had directed it, or striven to direct it, in the great crises of its history; in the midst of crooked and perverse generations they had stood as light-bearers, holding aloft the word of life; had ever stood for God and truth and right. In company with their religious songs, the words of the prophets were the nation's most cherished literature; their deeds were its heroics. Each incident of the life of each, from Moses to "the messenger" Malachi, retained its perennial interest for the people, as they heard them read or related them to their children.

Like massive trees along the horizon-line of the centuries the prophets stood ;—trees which had drawn up into themselves the sap and influences of their times ; which also, on the upward side, had expanded in the light and warmth and purity of a divinely vitalising atmosphere, and whose leaves and fruit had been for the healing of the people.

To this heritage of history, and into this environment of his nation's life, and thought, and circumstances,—its gloomy present, its smouldering hopes, its exalted ideal, as yet apparently afar off,—was John the Baptist born, the last, as he was the greatest, of the prophets,—"yea, and more than a prophet."

CHAPTER I

HOME LIFE

TO the Hebrews, the denial of offspring was "sorrow's crown of sorrow." Besides the disappointment of a natural instinct, it had come to be regarded as an affliction, a reproach, a possible evidence of Jehovah's displeasure. It meant, moreover, the extinction of their branch of the family in the national records, a prospect undesirable and depressing to any one, but especially so to those to whom continuance of lineage was connected with the highest hope of their race. For there was at least the possibility, though the probability amounted to the smallest fraction, that if children were given, they might be in the line of ancestry of the Messiah, while childlessness meant, of course, that for them the very possibility was blotted out.

When Zacharias the priest, "of the course of Abia,"[1] and Elisabeth his wife, were "advanced in their days"[2]—"far gone,"[3] that is, as to the hope of offspring, and the hope itself, long deferred, at last had withered, their hearts were suddenly gladdened by the expectation of a child. New heavens and a new earth opened to them when their son was born. The softened haze of disappointment which had gathered upon the late afternoon of their lives dispersed, the day brightened up again, and at eventide it was light.

Like Isaac and Samuel, John was a child born out of due time, and, in accordance with the prevalent belief, was received by his parents, and by all "the hill country of Judea," as a remarkable

---

[1] 1 Chron. xxiii.   [2] προβεβηκότες.   [3] See Note A.

child, one full of promise and divine purpose, one from whom extraordinary things might be expected,—"fear came on all them that dwelt round about them," and they said, "What then shall this child be?" In that quiet village home there came a reverent bending of thankful hearts before Jehovah as the grey-haired father and mother leaned over the child's cot, for the happiness of hopes realised at last and the new life given; and especially for the honourable position he should hold in the kingdom of God. He shall "be called the prophet of the Highest," shall "go before the face of the Lord to prepare His ways," and "give knowledge of salvation unto His people by the remission of their sins."

The current of their life's interest runs in a new channel; "a little child leads them." Hitherto it has run in the bed of sacred scrolls and priestly service in the Temple, but there is a new factor now; a living God's epistle daily before them; a light which, as it feebly burns in the new lamp, is, at least in their eyes, a beam of the light Eternal, a veritable Shekinah telling of God's presence *there*. The honour of it is almost too great, for he belongs more to God than to them, and yet to them is committed his training for high and holy service. In the sombre landscape of their lives a garden has been made, and they feel the privilege, and responsibility too, of dressing and keeping it. With what timid concern they watch him and minister to his wants! with what anxious carefulness they eradicate its weeds, almost fearing as they do it!

And they were worthy of their high calling and sacred charge. The brief description of St. Luke is perfect in its simplicity: "they were both of them righteous as in the presence of God, walking in all the commandments and observances of the Lord blameless." The ageing pair have

> "Grown together,
> Like to a double cherry";

and with mutual accord do they maintain, in "doing justly, loving mercy, and walking humbly with God," consciences "void of offence toward God and man."

Nothing is lacking to the picture : we see the reposeful village, the neat, orderly home, the quiet and regular ways of its inmates, their kindly humanity, their "hearts at leisure from themselves, to soothe and sympathise," calm souls who reverenced God, His Word, and His House, and who, waiting upon Him, accepted His providences with unquestioning acquiescence or with thankfulness. With them the rites and ceremonies of their religion are not a function, they are a privilege and a life. Within them and about them is that other-worldliness, that sweetness and light, which can, which alone can, instil and foster in their child truth, purity, love, and the fear of God.

It was this atmosphere of reverence, conscientiousness, and refinement, which John breathed from the first. He belonged to the choicest *caste* of the chosen people, using the word without its stigma. The son of a priestly race,—a race which held the chief and most unquestioned position in the nation,—he inherited its seclusive tendencies, and to his opening mind its quiet and retirement must have been congenial. He was of the priestly race on both sides, for his mother was "of the daughters of Aaron." Heredity and its bias count for much in the inclination of the developing life. The fineness of grain that comes from a godly and cultured ancestry, especially when there is no concern about the basal questions, "What shall we eat, what shall we drink, and wherewithal shall we be clothed?" constitutes a mental and spiritual capital of the golden denomination, a capital whose value can hardly be over-estimated.

But if transmission of good qualities and virtuous instincts count for much, environment, instruction, and discipline count for at least as much. When, however, all four are on the same plane and in the same line, the three latter consolidating and developing the former, the resultant must be a strong, sound, and manly character.

We can also imagine what springs of moral and religious

influence poured their waters into the growing river of his life before it reached the boundaries of the home domain. The instruction he received was one of them. Not upon broad: upon narrow, well-defined, incisive lines would that teaching be. In it there would be no recognition of culture or letters outside the Hebrew people; in all probability the literature of other countries was quite unknown in the old priest's home. Even if Zacharias knew of it, it would be to him profane, in the purest meaning of the word—outside the temple, secular, common; while only inside the temple of the Law and the Prophets could the highest truth, divine truth, be found.[1] The sacred records contained everything it most concerned them to know; all things needful for life and godliness were there. They formed John's first reading books. And even long before he could read them at all, his memory had encompassed The Ten Words, written by the very finger of God, the kernel of the Law; just as our children commit to memory the Lord's Prayer.

John's recollections in after years would be of the constant perusal by his father of the sacred books, and of his patient teaching of their contents to him. To no ordinance of the Lord was the devout Hebrew parent more faithful than to that which enjoined the careful catechising of his children in the first principles of their faith and first records of their history: "These

[1] Even the broadly-educated Josephus, in writing against Apion (Bk. I. sec. 8), makes it a strong point that they, the Jews, had not many books to study. "For we have not an innumerable multitude of books among us, disagreeing from and contradicting one another (as the Greeks have), but only twenty-two books, which contain the records of all the past times; which are justly believed to be divine; and of them five belong to Moses, which contain his laws, and the traditions of the origin of mankind till his death." As showing the high regard in which the people held their sacred books, the historian continues: "And how firmly we have given credit to those books of our own nation, is evident by what we do; for, during so many ages as have already passed, no one has been so bold as either to add anything to them, or take anything from them, or to make any change in them; for it becomes natural to all Jews, immediately and from their very birth, to esteem those books to contain divine doctrines, and to persist in them, and, if occasion be, willingly to die for them."

words shall be in thine heart, and thou shalt teach them diligently to thy children, and thou shalt talk of them when thou sittest in thine house, and when thou walkest by the way, and when thou liest down, and when thou risest up" (Deut. vi. 6, 7).[1]

Family worship is also a strong and sacred power. We can almost see the small group in the eventide reverently laying aside other duties, while "the sire turns o'er wi' patriarchal grace," or rather unrolls, some copy of the Law or one of the Prophets :

> "The priest-like father reads the sacred page,
> How Abram was the friend of God on high ;
> Or Moses bade eternal warfare wage
> With Amalek's ungracious progeny ;
> Or how the royal bard did groaning lie,
> Beneath the stroke of heaven's avenging ire ;
> Or Job's pathetic plaint and wailing cry ;
> Or rapt Isaiah's wild, seraphic fire ;
> Or other holy seers that tune the sacred lyre."[2]

When able to read for himself, the idyllic tales that fascinated us in our childhood hold him in still deeper fascination. For he was nearer them, and the blood of his own race was in the veins of those who acted, not their mimic, but their serious parts, in those great dramas that were often tragedies. "Sons of God," they seemed, in the perspective of history, close enough to Jehovah to talk with Him ; while, in the inverted perspective of reverential imagination, they loomed so large upon the horizon as to overtop and belittle the men of nearer times.

The Hebrew people have always been strong upon the poetic

---

[1] Again we may adduce the testimony of Josephus. "Our principal care " says he, " is this, to educate our children well ; and we think it to be the most necessary business of our whole life, to observe the laws that have been given us, and to keep those rules of piety that have been delivered down to us." And again : "It (the Law) also commands us to bring the children up in learning, and to exercise them in the laws, and make them acquainted with the acts of their predecessors, in order to their imitation of them, and that they may be nourished up in the laws from their infancy, and might neither transgress them nor yet have any pretence for their ignorance of them."

[2] Burns, *The Cottar's Saturday Night*.

side, and there is much in the story of their race that spontaneously lends itself to this treatment,—much of heroic faith; of walking with God, not knowing whither they walked; of sublime victory or pathetic captivity; and, above all, there is that religious truth and those observances around which their highest aspirations and deepest reverence clung,—the presence of Jehovah among them, and the sanctities of His worship. Loved and prized by all were "Those strains that once did sweet in Zion glide." And as children naturally fall to poetry, for the world to them is still poetic, John would certainly store in his memory those psalms and poetic compositions in history and prophecy which still form a large part of the choicest and most valuable spiritual heritage of mankind.

He reads the story of his race from the calling of its founder; follows with absorbent mind and burning heart each vicissitude of its career, now rejoicing at a victory, now subdued at a defeat, now sympathetic in some cruel oppression or dark captivity; while slowly the deep meaning and divine purpose of its election shape themselves before him. He read with sorrow and anger both, of the times when they forsook Jehovah, and other, foreign, gods were worshipped by his people: but his soul glowed with admiration at the heroic stand made by the prophets in face of kings and people;—their fearless reproofs; their holding aloft the standard of a divine righteousness that would not lower its sanctions to meet the lowered tone of the nation's morality; their passionate exhortations to return; and all in face of ingratitude and the danger of imprisonment and martyrdom itself. Ever would one dramatic scene draw his eyes, like the chief incident in a powerful picture,—that of his great prototype, as, single-handed, he stood on the promontory of Carmel before the angry king, the host of false priests, and the multitudes of the people. Perhaps this was the best perused part of the scroll, this and the writings of the burning, rapt Isaiah.

To this growing youth of the thoughtful face and eyes that look beyond, there comes, as he ponders, the root idea of the kingdom of God: how that their nation was established and grew, was fenced around and administered, from the standpoint of Jehovah as its ruler and judge, in a word, as its Head; how that beneath all the earthly forms in which it was incarnated, often very imperfect and with grave moral defects, there were still the spiritual conception and heavenly purpose of its choosing, and the never-abdicated claims of Jehovah.

While as for the future, the kingdom still to come would find its centre and head in the King Messiah; around Him would be drawn the spiritual forces of the nation; He would "restore the kingdom to Israel," be the King of the Jews, bring in the glory of the golden age, and fully realise both the material and spiritual ideal. And his faith in the realisation of this vision grew in strength as the vision itself grew in beauty.

The neighbourhood in which he lived contributed the glow and power of its historic associations. This was "the hill-country of Judea," the Judean part, that is, of the southern hill-country of the land of Palestine. A study of the map of Canaan will show that the whole "hill-country" west of the Jordan was divided into two parts by the plain of Esdraelon. That to the north stretches away towards Mount Hermon and the Lebanon range, while that on the south gradually rises to Jerusalem and Hebron, then falls off into the broken land of the great wilderness. This latter portion forms an irregular parallelogram, having the Philistian plain on the west, and on the east the deep gorge of the Jordan, which opens, at its extremity, into the Lake Asphaltitis. The home of Zacharias was in one of the small towns that dotted the valleys or crowned the hills of that part of this tract which was within the territory of the tribe of Judah. The name of the "city" has not been given us. It has been conjectured [1] to be Juttah, and the suggestion added that we should read Juttah instead of Juda in the text. But, in the first place, no scribe or copyist would be likely to make such a substitution of letters as this would imply, by a slip of the pen; and, in the second, the

[1] Reland, *Palestine*.

reading Juda is not called in question by any of the manuscripts. We should not therefore be justified in altering it simply on the ground of semblance.

It may have been Juttah for anything we know to the contrary, for this was one of the "cities with their suburbs" assigned to the priests (Josh. xxi. 16), and it was "in the mountains" (Josh. xv. 48, 55). It certainly was one of the priestly cities. And with its "suburbs" carefully and well cultivated (for priests mostly make good gardeners), laid out in orchards and vineyards, it must have been a charmingly quiet place to live in. Go out from which gate you would, the eye rested on trimly-kept vines and peaceful pastures; in spring the air was fragrant with the scent of blossoms; in autumn the numberless trees of olive, fig, pomegranate, and the rest, vied with each other in bringing forth their fruit in their season.

There is nothing more inducive both of observation and of thought than "dressing and keeping" a garden; its occupations contribute a gentle stimulus, rather than a check, to the calmness of contemplation; for while there is always something to be done, and opportunities cannot be missed without penalty, yet, on the other hand, Nature cannot be hurried, she will have her own time in developing and ripening her gifts. And the mystery of life, and the miracle of multiplication, constantly before the cultivator's eyes, can hardly fail to raise his thought to Him by whom both are given. If John assisted his father in these pursuits, as probably he did, he would find them a plastic matrix in which his thoughts and visions, tending to coherence, became embedded.

The country round about was replete with historic connection. It was indissolubly linked with the great names of the nation. About these rounded hills and through these pleasant valleys the patriarchs themselves had led their flocks. Along one or other of these roads the merchant caravan had gone down into Egypt, bearing "spicery, balm, and myrrh," and all unwittingly had, in the person of Joseph, borne the destiny of the nation too; along the same Jacob's sons had returned to fetch their aged father. In that direction had David fled, and among those hills "every one in distress, or in debt, or discontented, gathered themselves unto him, and he became a captain over them." And there were a hundred associations besides.

Hebron could not be far away. It is a city of great antiquity, one of the oldest in the world, in fact. Close at hand was the cave of Machpelah, keeping guard over its sacred treasures, the graves of the three patriarchs and their wives. The history of the city was interwoven with great names and critical times. From Hebron Jacob sent the son of his old age to seek his brethren, a small event which proved to be the pivot on which turned the early history of the chosen race. The spies from the children of Israel in their wanderings visited it, and reported it to be in the possession of the Anakim. At the division of the country among the tribes it was allotted to Judah, afterwards becoming one of the six cities of refuge, and a Levitical city. Under David it resumed its state as a royal town, until the fortress of Jebus was taken and Jerusalem became the centre of his government. At one time it was the ecclesiastical centre of the nation: so that by the time of John it had come to hold a relationship to Jerusalem, and a reputation, in some respects similar to that which Canterbury now holds to London.

Living in such a home, and with such a disposition, he must have made frequent visits to Jerusalem, either with his father, or making one in the caravans of pilgrims which went up at the yearly feasts, going "from strength to strength," one company joining another as they debouched from the valleys and converged toward Jerusalem, until they all "appeared before God in Zion." It is not possible for us with our Western education to fully comprehend the "burning of the heart" which John, or indeed any devout Hebrew, felt as he neared the sacred city, and at length stood within the gloom of the great Temple. God is everywhere, a Spirit, and they who worship Him in spirit and in truth can worship Him everywhere with equal confidence of acceptance. Wherever there is a heart to pray, there is a God ready to hear and to bless. But it was otherwise to the Jew. He came behind none in his belief in the Divine omnipresence.

> "If I climb up into heaven, Thou art there;
> Should I make Sheol my bed, behold, Thou art there.
> If I take the wings of the morning,
> If I dwell in the uttermost parts of the sea;
> Even there shall Thy hand lead me,
> And Thy right hand shall hold me." (Ps. cxxxix. 8–10.)

But it was at that spot which Jehovah had "chosen to place His name there" that He was, to the belief of the Jew, to be especially and properly worshipped. There was His "real Presence." When standing in the Temple before the veil, the devout worshipper felt that only just behind it was the actual, personal presence of the God of Abraham, Isaac, and Jacob—the God of his fathers, and the Creator of the ends of the earth. No other, of all the places of prayer throughout the land, had the sanctions, or the nearness to Jehovah, of this one. It was as if we should regard every place of worship with one exception, throughout town and country—cathedral, church, chapel, meeting-house —as simply human institutions under divine sanction, for instruction in religious things and the development of the spiritual life; that exception being, let us suppose, Westminster Abbey, where, once a year, God revealed Himself "behind the veil."

If we could conceive this, and could imagine the feelings of a serious and earnest youth as he waited and prayed outside the Temple with the vast multitude, "on the great day, the day of atonement," while he knew that inside the still warm blood of the goat was being sprinkled on the altar as the confession of the right of life forfeited through sin, and the supplication for Divine mercy; if we could imagine the hushed and reverent awe which overspread the whole assembly as they felt that God was very near, attending to their prayers and supplications, the movement of relief as the priest came out to bless them in the name of the Lord, we could then imagine the deep impression which must have been made upon the soul of John by this central act of his nation's religion.

Through all the years which this brief sketch covers, the development of the soul of John proceeded ; "the hand of the Lord was with him," "he waxed strong in spirit" ; and we must not forget that through it all, too, he had the kindly direction and careful explanation of his father, who rejoiced in the strengthening spirit of his son. The seed is sown "in an honest and good heart," for lifelong growth and fruitage.

CHAPTER II

"IN THE DESERTS"

IN the meagreness of the historic record, no mention is made of the occasion on which John definitely left his home and betook himself to the open country of the southern borderland. But most probably it was on the death of one of his now aged parents. As a Nazirite, he was not to "come near to a dead body." " He shall not make himself unclean," said the law, "for his father, or for his mother, for his brother, or for his sister, when they die, because his separation unto God is upon his head."[1] And if we suppose that he afterwards returned home, it would be but for the short while his other parent lived; on whose death he, having no near relations or close personal friends, for he was, and probably always had been, of a solitary habit, and having, moreover, his manner of life shaped out for him, partly by his vow, and partly by those growing thoughts within him which drove him out, would finally leave "the hill country of Judea." Then he made his dwelling-place far from the homes and haunts of men, among "the deserts and mountains, and dens and caves of the earth."[2]

[1] Num. vi. 7.

[2] Robertson (of Brighton) adduces John's dissatisfaction with the state of religion among the people as the probable reason of his withdrawal. He says: "It was a period, probably, in which, saddened by the hollowness of all life in Israel, and perplexed with the controversies of Jerusalem, the controversies of Sadducee with Pharisee, of formalist with mystic, of the disciples of one infallible Rabbi with the disciples of another infallible Rabbi, he fled for refuge to the wilderness, to see whether God could not be found by the heart that sought Him, without the aid of churches, rituals, creeds, or forms."

John has now definitely entered upon the second great stage of his preparation. No more will there be for him bright looks of love, nor the bliss of love returned, nor any offices of affection, no family interests, no social intercourse, no home, not even a sheltering roof.

He took his solitary way toward "the boundless region of treeless downs" which stretched southward far beyond the reach of the eye to the great desert where the chosen people wandered in hardship after their Egyptian bondage, a desolation of broken country, verily "a great and terrible wilderness." On the east this silent land terminates in the barren shores and ill-omened waters of Lake Asphaltitis, or the Dead Sea, and on the northeast the limit is reached at the small town of Engedi. Prof. Palmer gives us graphic descriptions of this region, over which, it is all but certain, John's feet must often have trod. "The wilderness of Engedi,"[1] says he, "is as grand but dreary a sight as can well be imagined: a broad rolling expanse shut in on every hand by high ridges with jagged summits, their sides deeply scored by torrent-beds, and intersected here and there by broad valleys of white marl, with not a tree, and scarcely a shrub, to be seen for miles around. From time to time a small Arab encampment or a few isolated figures come in sight, and, with their primeval costume, and their wild and savage air, seem like some weird vision of David and his outlaw band conjured up by a highly-wrought fancy, rather than the ordinary inhabitants of the place." "At length we stand," says the same authority, "upon the shores of the Dead Sea, the frightful desolation of which accords well with the terrible history that attaches to the spot. We are undoubtedly in the neighbourhood of the Cities of the Plain. . . . Many writers have supposed that the agencies employed in the destruction of Sodom and its sister cities were the natural ones of volcanic eruptions accompanied by earthquake. This hypothesis is quite in accordance with the language of the Bible; the mention in Genesis of slime (*i.e.* asphalt) pits in the

[1] *Picturesque Palestine.*

neighbourhood, and of Abraham's seeing that 'the smoke of the country went up as the smoke of a furnace,' would certainly seem to indicate such phenomena. The asphalt pits are still to be seen, and the frequent and severe earthquakes that have occurred in the vicinity also point to the presence of subterranean volcanic action."[1]

This scene must have struck the mind of John, which turned more naturally to judgment than to mercy, as a powerful evidence of the avenging hand of the Almighty. As he looked upon the broken, black, bituminous region, it would seem as if the iniquities of those old, lost, accursed cities had eaten into the very soil, making it barren and desolate for ever.

John had been partly schooled and prepared for the rigours of his desert life by his training as a Nazirite. According to "the prophecies which went before on him," he was to "drink no wine nor strong drink, and to be filled with the Holy Ghost from his mother's womb." The Nazirites were not a community; their vows and obligations were personal only, and in the case of "Nazirites of days," whose vows were but temporarily assumed and for some special purpose, were terminable according to the will or conscience of each. Anyone could become a Nazirite, and at any time, and need not even leave his daily avocation unless he wished. Of this kind was St. Paul's vow in Cenchræa, and that of those for whom he became "at charges" in Jerusalem, "declaring the fulfilment of the days of purification until the offering was offered for every one of them." These characteristics mark out the Nazirite as distinctive from the Essene community of John's own day; they also demonstrate that his asceticism was not the same in basis with the monkish brotherhoods of later centuries. But there was another class of Nazirites, those

[1] Recent years have furnished us with a graphic illustration of a sudden catastrophe of the kind probably which overwhelmed the Cities of the Plain. In June 1886, there occurred that eruption of Mount Tarawera, New Zealand, which destroyed the famous Pink and White Terraces of Lake Rotomahana, and converted, in a few hours, a whole region, lovely as the garden of Eden, into a scene of utter ruin.

who were such "for life." The nature of the vows appears to have been the same in both cases, the only difference being in their duration. They were regarded as of peculiar sacredness and binding force: "there was a sacramental consecration of the whole life to God." The ceremonies connected therewith bear a striking resemblance to those employed in the consecration of the high priest himself.[1]

The root-principle of the Naziritic vow was the dedication, in such cases as that of John, i.e. in lifelong cases, of the whole nature and untouched life to the service of Jehovah; a life to be kept free from external taint of impurity, or defilement by contact with the corruption of death; while its inward purity and sensitiveness should be such as to catch the most delicate indications of Jehovah's will. The soul, like some high mountain, was to lift itself and maintain itself in the clear, pure atmosphere of heaven.

The rule of the vow was threefold—to allow the hair to grow; not to touch any dead body; and to drink neither wine nor strong drink. The first was the chief public evidence of the vow. It marked the Nazirite out as distinct from his fellows, and formed the pledge, the outward and visible sign, of an inward and spiritual consecration. And by it the profession was made, that the head, the seat of those great faculties which constitute the special honour of manhood, and in which the very image of God inheres, was separated from the world's rough interests, dedicated to meditate upon divine truth, and if called upon, to proclaim it in strong unswerving speech.

The second has been already mentioned—he was not to come in contact with the dead. "The tendencies at work in each of these institutions (Nazarites and Essenes) are," says Dr. Reynolds,

---

[1] As showing the high and sacred value inherent in the vow of the Nazirite, it is noteworthy that the word translated "crown," in connection with the High Priest (נֵזֶר) in Lev. xxi. 12, is the same as that which, in Num. vi. 18, denotes the long hair of the Nazirite. Consult the whole section in *Aids to the Student*, in the Queen's Printer's Bible.

"each of them expressions of a deep-seated conviction that the deliverance of the whole man from evil is almost identical with the deliverance of the spirit from the power or contamination of the flesh. They rest upon the thesis which has ever exerted signal influence over the Oriental mind, that the seat of evil is not in the soul nor the will so much as in the flesh of man; that the flesh derives its corruption from the main physical and material conditions; that the material universe is the *evil* principle." While, as to the individual, evil was believed to have its seat, not in the soul itself, but in that flesh which forms for a time its habitation, and through which it is related to the material world. The flesh therefore is the enemy of the spirit, clogs it, drags it down; it must be fought against and vanquished, that the soul may rise untrammelled into that high region of freedom and peace which is essential to communion with the divine.

There is, of course, much truth in this position. The flesh with its affections and lusts must be kept under. The two laws which are at war within our members have ever been recognised as the first fact of moral introspection, while the obligation to follow the higher is one of the fundamentals of all religion. Yet it falls much below the standard of Jesus and the New Testament. It fails to recognise that all evil whatsoever goes behind the flesh, and takes its rise in the immaterial thought or passion or will. It is "out of the *heart* that evil thoughts, murders, adulteries, fornications, thefts, false witness, railings"—"the things which defile a man"—come forth.

Neither does it take into account that our bodies can be presented as living sacrifices to God, that they are meant in the divine intention to be veritable temples and shrines "of the Holy Spirit." It belongs to the higher region of Christian ethics to see that the world, with its numberless scenes and things of beauty, is not a waste, howling wilderness, but a real God's world, pronounced "very good" at its creation; to see that the body is not to be despised, contemned, and weakened, but that, like a young and spirited horse, it is to be so broken-in, that it passions, the chief elements of its danger, may, under control, give strength to goodness and vigour to activity; to see, again, that life, in the world as the theatre, and through the body as the instrument, may, by its experiences, discipline the spirit until its dross shall be purged away and it shall grow into the lineaments of the lost image.

We do not, of course, condemn John for not knowing those things which belong to a later and fuller revelation, and respecting which " he that is least in the kingdom of heaven is greater than he." We simply indicate our higher privilege. To the Baptist, the body was to be repressed; life, with its thousand-fold interests and sacred human affections, formed a strong cage which had caught and prisoned for a while the human soul in its progress upward.

This whole doctrine of ascetic renunciation has an intense power within its own limits, like a mountain torrent whose impetuous force is in proportion to the narrowness of its channel. Yet it indicates a line of life which all cannot follow; neither is it divinely intended all should: such a life belongs rather to those who are selected for a special purpose, and to whom it will afford the best possible training. But from this doctrine as premise, the conclusion logically follows that the spirit must fight relentlessly against the flesh, which is a " body of death," hindering, oppressing, dragging it down at every point. When, therefore, the spirit has left the body, the body, repellent in itself even while in life, seems tenfold more so, as it is the cold and vanquished enemy which retained its vindictiveness to the last.

As for the Baptist, we know from the story how resolutely he maintained the fight against the flesh, how he kept his body under, reducing his wants to the simplest and their supply to the roughest, by means of which, and devout contemplation, he put the world beneath his feet, and moved on that high plane where it becomes self-evident that the things which are seen are temporary and the things not seen eternal.

Abstinence from wine and strong drink formed the third

essential of the Nazirite; total abstinence—" no vinegar of wine, or vinegar of strong drink, neither shall he drink any liquor of grapes, nor eat fresh grapes or dried," " nothing that is made of the grape-vine, from the kernel to the husk." [1]

It seems at first sight somewhat strange that the vine, the symbol to the Hebrews of heavenly favour and earthly prosperity, and used in their sacred writings as the illustration of Jehovah's especial care,[2] should be placed under the ban, but the reason becomes more evident the more we consider it.

The action of wine and strong drink on the human system is not to "prepare," to "make straight," "the way of the Lord" into the soul of the prophet, but to make it crooked and to break it up. Wine and strong drink disturb the cool and even currents of the mind; so stimulating the activity of the brain as to promise greater nimbleness to thought, and brighter visions to the imagination. But wine-spurred faculties do not evolve the truest thought: if quicker for a time, it is less firm in its step, and though the pictures of the imagination may be brighter in their colouring, their outlines are blurred and their colours meretricious. In no such case is the calm ethical ideal apprehended. And further, the seat itself of the faculties rapidly degenerates under repeated stimulation, becoming less and less fit for the Almighty to employ in revealing Himself to man, to say nothing of the general physical and moral deterioration which ensues and makes the unfitness more pronounced. For a prophet, then, to keep altogether clear of wine and strong drink was to maintain the bodily powers and mental faculties at their best, and to preserve that pure heart wherewith to see God and His truth.

In many old religions, wine, because of its stimulating effects, was supposed to bestow inspiration; to make those who brought themselves into an intoxicated condition, the media through which the gods spoke to men. The human will was placed *hors de combat*, that the god might borrow and use the faculties.

[1] Num. vi. 3, 4. [2] As *e.g.* Isa. v.

"Wild excitement stimulated by wine was supposed to confer the highest revelations."[1] *In vino veritas* had more than a social application; it had a religious meaning. Hence the position wine held in the religious ceremonies of the Greeks, Romans, and Orientals. Among the former the worship of Bacchus is well known, while among the Vedic peoples we read of the glorification of the soma-juice.

> "We've quaffed the soma bright, and are immortal grown;
> We've entered into light, and all the gods have known."[2]

This idea of the intimate connection of divinity and wine was so widespread and so unquestioned, that it was at once applied to the inspirational possession of the Holy Spirit on the day of Pentecost, which, though shortly after John, illustrates the prevalent belief of the time—"These men are full of new wine." This was the attribution St. Peter most strenuously resisted, refuting it by the statement that it was the fulfilment of Joel's prophecy, "I will pour out *my spirit* upon all flesh, and your sons and your daughters shall prophesy."

There is the same juxtaposition of wine and the Spirit, but with a *non licet* as to the stimulant, in the case of John—"He shall drink neither *wine nor strong drink*, and he shall be filled with the *Holy Spirit* from his mother's womb"; and also in St. Paul's exhortation to the Ephesians—"Be not *drunk with wine*," do not seek your spiritual power and inspiration there, "but be filled with the *Spirit*."

Thus carefully do the sacred writers guard that vinous excitation shall not be confounded with the possession of the divine Spirit. The strongest condemnation is implied on the drunken prophet—"The priest and the prophet have erred through strong

---

[1] Reynolds' *John the Baptist*.
[2] It is but fair to say that this is not their highest teaching. The fourth rule of the highest road of the eightfold path is:—
> "Shun drugs and drinks which work the wit abuse;
> Clean minds, clean bodies, need no soma-juice."
> Arnold's *Light of Asia*.

drink, they are swallowed up of wine," "they err in vision and stumble in judgment." [1]

Especially, then, must the prophet keep himself pure, that with clear eyes he may look on truth through no distorting or colouring media, and therefore untruly, but in the direct and achromatic light of the Sun of Righteousness.

The general principles of asceticism are of necessity somewhat similar. And from the rigours of John's life in the desert it has been argued that he belonged to the Essenic brotherhood. But there are "no traits handed down which suggest that he was a member of the Essene community. He was an ascetic, and the Essenes were ascetics; but this is plainly an inadequate basis for any such inference." "His abode was the desert; his clothing was rough; his food was spare; he baptised his penitents. Therefore, it is argued, he was an Essene. Between the premisses and the conclusion, however, there is a broad gulf, which cannot very easily be bridged over. The solitary, independent life which John led presents a type wholly different from the cenobitic establishments of the Essenes, who had common property, common meals, common hours of labour and of prayer. It may even be questioned whether his food of locusts would have been permitted by the Essenes, if they really ate nothing which had life. And again, his baptism, as related by the Evangelists, and their lustrations as described by Josephus, have nothing in common except the use of water for a religious purpose. . . . If positive statements are allowable, it would be more true to fact to say that he could not possibly have been an Essene. The rule of his life was *isolation;* the principle of theirs, *community*." [2]

But to what continuous severities is the Evangelist's brief description the index-finger:—"John had his raiment of camel's hair, and a leathern girdle about his loins, and his food was

---

[1] Isa. xxviii. 7.

[2] Dr. Lightfoot. The whole subject of the Essenes is most ably and exhaustively dealt with in the Dissertation at the end of his indispensable Commentary on Colossians and Philemon.

locusts and wild honey." His long garment had no suggestion of comfort in it : durable in wear and coarse in texture, such as only the poorest wore, such as the dervishes wear to this day, it was the sharpest antithesis of the "soft raiment in kings' houses." Locusts were specially and by name exempted from the law of the unclean—"Every creeping thing that flieth is unclean to you. . . . Yet these may ye eat of all winged creeping things . . . the locust after its kind, the bald locust after its kind, and the cricket after its kind, and the grasshopper after its kind."[1] Burckhardt, quoted in Thomson's *The Land and the Book*, says that "the Arabs, in preparing locusts as an article of food, throw them alive into boiling water with which a good deal of salt has been mixed. After a few minutes they are taken out and dried in the sun ; the head, feet, and wings are then torn off; the bodies are cleansed from the salt and perfectly dried, after which process whole sacks are filled with them by the Bedawîn. They are sometimes eaten boiled with butter, and they often contribute materials for a breakfast when spread over unleavened bread mixed with butter." Thomson continues that they are "tolerated only by the very poorest people. John the Baptist, however, was of this class. . . . His ordinary 'meat' was dried locusts—probably fried in butter and mixed with honey, as is still frequently done. . . . Wild honey is still gathered in large quantities from trees in the wilderness, and from rocks in the wadies, just where the Baptist sojourned."[2][3] The principle of the whole is, that John reduced his wants to the barest and simplest necessities, in order to "keep his body under," and also to have as few points of contact as possible with the world of men.

[1] Lev. xi. 20-23.   [2] See 1 Sam. xiv.
[3] "In the Ebionitic recension of Matthew, we find the food of John described as μέλι ἄγριον, οὗ ἡ γεῦσις ἦν τοῦ μάννα, ὡς ἐγκρὶς ἐν ἐλαίῳ ('it had the taste of manna, as a cake baked in oil,' Num. xi. 8). The simple statement of Matthew is here misrepresented, and even falsified. The ἀκρίδες (locusts) seemed to this writer food unworthy for John, and he makes ἐγκρίδες (cakes) of them, and thus gets a chance of comparing John's food with manna."—Neander's *Life of Christ*.

Consider, then, the dreary monotony of his life in this wilderness,—his companions the wild beasts, whom he watched as they pursued and pounced upon their prey, whose daily habits, as they stole along the hillsides or hid among the rocks, became familiar to him, and who on their part came to know the anchorite and did not molest him. Each day passed like its predecessor, neither was there any change or incident to look forward to on the morrow. The sun rose out of the grey haze over the bare mountains in the east, became a burnished and burning ball for the day, then sank into the purple gloom of the west.

"The sun went down, the stars rushed out,
At one stride came the dark,"

and with it the deep indigo sky, "inlaid with patines of bright gold," while now and again the echoing scream of a bird, or the cry of a jackal, seemed rather to emphasise the stillness than to break it, as a flash of lightning in the night seems to intensify the darkness.

With such habits and amid such surroundings, the growing prophet lived for long, uneventful years.

CHAPTER III

"The Thought that Breathes"

THERE are three heavens for men, even on the earth. The first is that of material success and prosperity, in which there is no further concern as to answering the great basal questions of food and clothing, and in whose charmed circles there are delightful social relationships. The second is that of philosophic calm, whose enjoyments are found in balanced thought, advancing knowledge, and cultured taste,—whose realm is literature, science, or art, or all. The third is that which rises, like some mountain peak above the smoke, above the cloud, into the still pure heavens, upon whose Sinai summit divine truth is revealed, unspeakable words are heard; on which Jehovah Himself descends to declare His imperishable law.

It was in the third, the highest, that John the Baptist lived during those monotonous desert years. The Almighty prepares His choicest servants by the discipline of solitude. He is not afraid to throw them back upon bare, solid, fundamental truths: He has faith enough in them to know that they will not falter nor fail when the spirit passes before them, and they behold "the face of Immortality unveiled." Only in solitude can heaven and earth, the eternal and the temporal, God and humanity, righteousness and the wrongs of men, be adequately apprehended or their mutual relationships truly adjusted. While daily cares, household or business anxieties, are incessantly alighting on the balances, it is not possible rightly to weigh these greatest truths. They require removal to such a distance that there shall not even be the trembling of the floor which comes from the traffic of the street. So large are they that both hands need to be emptied of other things to take effective hold on them. Let both be preoccupied with earth's affairs, and they remain unheeded altogether, like the crown in the hand of the angel above the head of the man with the rake ; if one hand tries to take hold, and the other be engaged with matters merely mundane, the grasp is apt to slacken in the interest of the things that are seen, when the greater truths take wing and fly away. It is necessary to withdraw, at least now and again, from "the loud, stunning tide"; to come "into the desert places and rest awhile."

The "desert" places,—where the thought is driven inward. As Isaac Taylor puts it :—"There is a purity or abstinence in the tastes of the man of 'spiritual' education which forbids that he should desire to be placed in the midst of the gaudy magnificence of nature, before he can fill his soul with the ravishments he delights in. He does not covet as his home some valley of the East where the sun seems to linger to shed all his favours. On the contrary, he would much rather draw his devout inferences from the slenderest or most modest examples ; he chooses to dwell upon instances where the parsimony of nature gives larger scope to the diligence of reflection, and where the premisses are always less obtrusive than the conclusion. It is most true that the pious contemplatist finds, in the sere herbage of the wilderness, and on the rugged and scorched surface of granite rocks, symbols enough of God." [1]

In the clear, dry atmosphere of the wilderness, the cubes of truth retain the sharpness of their edges, while in the busy world, with its thousand crossing and recrossing interests, the subtlety and speciousness of its evil, the edges are apt to be rubbed off, until at length the cubes will roll in compromise. Moreover, away from the haunts of men comes no false glamour arising from pleasure, or success, or ambitious contest ; these things fade till they seem of no account.

[1] *Saturday Evening* : "The Recluse."

There, the being and the righteousness of God appear to be, as indeed they are, as far above "the little lives of men," as the interstellar spaces are greater than the small world we inhabit.

If we come to examine the record of their lives, we shall find that God's greatest servants have passed through such a period of silent mental incubation. For forty days and nights Moses stayed upon the sacred mount before he received the two tables of the law ; his prolonged and undistracted meditation so prepared him for apprehending the Almighty's glory, that his words, spoken in the name of heaven and earth's eternal King, and from Him, have had an incalculable influence in the moulding of the centuries. It was in the desert that "the still small voice" came to Elijah ; Jesus was "driven of the Spirit into the wilderness" for forty days after His baptism ; for three years Paul withdrew into quietude after his conversion. It is not surprising, then, that the Baptist's providential education should have the same great factor in it.

As we have seen, dreary must those solitudes have been to which John had exiled himself. Slowly the seasons went by. He braved the heat of the days and cold of the nights. He watched the thin bright green of the vegetation that crept, during and after the rainy season, along the valleys and up the sides of the hills, soon to change to brown under the fierce heat of the dry. He knew every path through the wilderness, — where the springs were ; where the wild bees made their nests, where the conies dwelt among the rocks ; he was "with the wild beasts," passing about unharmed, neither did they fear or fly at the approach of the silent, preoccupied recluse. But if he walked about half mechanically, he had no mechanical musing,—the fire burned ! The essential truths, the fundamental facts, Jehovah's supremacy, the sins and needs of his fellow-men, all stood out in sharp definition before his vision, revealed in the straight rays and white light of absolute truth. And into his fervent soul they settled, and at length amalgamated with it.

It is very probable that John took with him into the desert, when he definitely left his home, those sacred scrolls which had been his father's and now were his. For the furniture of the home he has no use; for these he has—they are treasures, essentials. In them his maturing spirit finds much in common with itself. The prophets were to the destined prophet kindred spirits. Let us then imagine John in his lonely cave, conning, with vivid imagination, the narratives of their heroic lives and faithful words, and, as he walked about, pondering them and their significance.

It is not easy for us, in these days, under this civilisation, and with our fuller body of truth, to gain the standpoint of the Baptist, and his outlook. But we must make the attempt. The Hebrew prophet was inspired by Jehovah, His spirit entered into him and clothed him. The Hebrew name "*Nabi*" recognises this passive aspect of the prophet as the recipient of the divine mind and will; it is from the passive form of the verb. "The root of the verb is said to be a word signifying to boil or bubble over, and is thus based upon the metaphor of a fountain bursting forth from the heart of man, into which God has poured it."[1]

In the stricter and more proper sense of the title, the prophets took their rise in Moses. They became an institution or order under Samuel, and continued under the kings. They were not circumscribed by heredity like the priestly order; anyone in whom dwelt the Spirit of God in sufficient measure, from whatever rank of life, was recognised and "established to be a prophet of the Lord." The gift was that of God, the recognition that of the people. They continued through the divided kingdom, through the Captivity, after it, until we come to Malachi. Through all the vicissitudes of their history Jehovah had not for long left Himself without a witness, until we come to the strange, long silence of the four hundred years between our "Testaments."

In regard to their religious teaching, its great characteristic was the proclamation of the Unity and Spirituality of the Divine Nature. To the Unity the prophets were ever faithful, lifting it up against those idolatries of surrounding nations which were not merely theoretical errors, but which, as every student knows, were

[1] Dean Stanley's *Jewish Church*, Lectures XIX. and XX.

so inwoven with their national life as to give the sanction of the gods to cruelties and immoralities simply horrible and unrelateable. The Spirituality of God, His justice, and His love, represented the active side of their teaching. "The moral manifestation of God in some impressive form constituted at once the first call and the sustaining force of every prophetic mission."

The prophets stood, too, to proclaim the inseparable union of morality with religion. There is hardly one of them whose life or writings does not contain an intense proclamation of this truth, as may be readily verified. "Mercy and justice, judgment and truth, repentance and goodness—not sacrifice, not fasting, not ablutions—is the burden of the whole prophetic teaching of the Old Testament." How unflinching were their denunciations of wrong, either in king, priest, or people; how powerful their appeals to the consciences of their fellow-countrymen! Sometimes they had been the leaders of the people, and always were they patriots. Indeed, they were essentially patriots. It was their function to bring back the nation to those strong moral foundations upon which alone it and its institutions could securely stand.

They saw visions and made predictions of a glorious future: but this will rise again for our consideration. The popular limitation of the idea of a prophet to a foreteller of future events, especially merely earthly events, is a quite erroneous and comparatively modern idea. That they did foretell such is of course without doubt, but the chief part of their work was to apply the principles of God's righteous rule to their time and nation. The religion of the Hebrews, as one of our calmest thinkers[1] writes, "gave existence to an inestimably precious unorganised institution, the order (if it may be so termed) of the prophets. Under the protection, generally though not always effectual, of their sacred character, the prophets were a power in the nation, often more than a match for kings and priests, and kept up, in that little corner of the earth, the antagonism of influences which is the only real security for continued progress. . . . The remark

[1] J. S. Mill, *Representative Government*.

of a distinguished Hebrew, that the prophets were in Church and State the equivalent of the modern liberty of the press, gives a just but not an adequate conception of the part fulfilled in national and universal history by this great element of Jewish life."

This meaning, this significance of the prophets and their function, was of course powerfully present to the mind of John out there in the solitude of the desert. Deeply did he ponder them, until he came to see the history of his people from their standpoint. Yet in all his retrospect he found no period wherein the prophet was more needed than his own. For four centuries—a period equal to that which stretches from the beginning of the reign of Henry the Eighth to our own time—the prophetic voice had been silent. No need is there for us to enter upon the weary intricacies,[1] the unworthy intrigues, the invasion of the heathen spirit with which the priesthood of the nation not only was powerless to cope, but which tainted it with its own consent, the gradual drawing on of a permanent captivity: it was a gloomy landscape, one of morasses, of "antres vast and deserts idle, rough quarries," with very few "rocks and hills whose heads touch heaven." Then he looked around upon the condition of his people in his own day. They are no longer a nation, their land is but a province bound to the triumphal car of Imperial Rome, and "they are slaves to those whom they believed themselves destined to rule." The eagles of the Cæsars fly in the air of the sacred city, and flout the Temple itself. His fellow-countrymen are treated by the conquerors with the calm contemptuousness of assured and unbreakable power. Mercilessly had they crushed patriotic insurrections, and they were quite prepared, if need be, to do so again. The land groaned beneath the oppressor's tread.

If politically the forward as well as the backward look was dark, it was still darker in the direction of religion. The sacred priesthood itself was corrupted into a political office. This must have been a point of special soreness to John, for, like Jeremiah

[1] See Introduction.

and Ezekiel, he was himself of the priestly order. It may be quite the fact that the exalted ideas we have been taught to attach to the priestly office did not belong to it in the Hebrew economy. It was for the most part and in most cases an external function. Personal character and life counted for little as to the validity of its duties; that was secured if they were officially and, from a ceremonial standpoint, properly performed. The man who held the office was subordinate—part of the apparatus. And the worship itself was a coarse one, external too, as compared with our ideas. "The arrangements of the temple were, as has been truly said, not those of a cathedral or a church, but of a vast slaughter-house, combined with a banqueting hall. Droves of oxen, sheep, and goats crowded the courts. Here were the rings to which they were fastened. There was the huge altar, towering above the people, on which the carcases were laid to be roasted. Underneath was the drain to carry off the blood. Close by was the apparatus for skinning and fleecing them. Round the court were kitchens for cooking the meat. The stench was abated by the fumigation of incense. For that which constitutes Christian devotion—prayer, praise, commemoration, exhortation—there was not in the Mosaic ritual any provision."[1]

It is very evident that John had but little regard for this aspect of the nation's religion. His was the prophetic, not the priestly, soul. The streaming blood was of infinitely less consequence to him than that state of heart which was a spiritual and living sacrifice. His attitude and position was that of his favourite Isaiah: "To what purpose is the multitude of your sacrifices unto Me? saith the Lord: I am full of the burnt offerings of rams, and the fat of fed beasts; and I delight not in the blood of bullocks, or of lambs, or of he goats. When ye come to appear before Me, who hath required this at your hand, to trample My courts . . . Wash you, make you clean; put away the evil of your doings from before Mine eyes; cease to do evil; learn to do well."[2]

[1] Stanley's *Jewish Church*, vol. ii. pp. 352-3. [2] Isa. i. 11-17.

Yet it is also evident that one of John's inwardness, a seeker into the heart and inner meaning of things, would, pushing aside the coarse externalism, recognise the spiritual import of it all. The central acts of a people's religion cannot be meaningless in their origin, nor spring from seed that is bad; their danger is that externalisms should so accumulate upon them that the life should go out by suffocation. And sacrifice meant sorrow for a broken law; it confessed the desert of punishment, even to the forfeiture of life; it sought to open an approach to God by a gift of the offerer, a gift valuable in proportion as it represented the entire dedication of the life. And as John's own life was a full dedication, he had seized the reality of which animal sacrifices were but the symbols.

Besides sacrifice, priesthood represented the line of approach of sinful man to his Maker. The priest appeared before God for him, and from God brought back forgiveness and blessing. He represented the people, in symbolism, to God. The high priest's very dress was a series of symbols, the gold plate on his forehead, on which was engraved the incommunicable Name, the breastplate with its twelve stones, the Urim and the Thummim. But the full purport of priesthood only came home to the mind of John when it was connected, as everything national was, with the hope of the Messiah. He would be the Lamb of God to bear away sin, led to the slaughter, the suffering Servant of Jehovah who should, through His consecrated pain and sorrow, enter into the mediatorial and administrative glory of His High Priesthood. Then we should see of the travail of His soul and be satisfied.

But the origin and the ideal, as against the present and the real, "what a fall was there!" The priesthood corrupted into a political office! It was "tampered with by Idumean tetrarchs or Roman procurators; the chief influence over the degraded Sanhedrin was in the hands of supple Herodians or wily Pharisees." Brooding over this contrast, the old warrior blood in the recluse was stirred. John did not forget that the "sons of Levi" had been essentially a military caste. As Dean Stanley points out, "every step of their early history is marked in blood! The consecration of the tribe was no calm ceremonial in the solitude of the sanctuary. It was by the tremendous self-dedication to the work of exterminating the worshippers of the molten calf." Their music was the clanging trumpet or the dissonant ram's horn. The morning hymn with which they raised the ark on their shoulders was the stirring war-cry: "Rise up, O Lord, and let Thine enemies be scattered." Nor did he forget that the greatest, the most heroic struggle his people could boast in their annals was led by a family of priests—the Maccabees, in whom seemed to be reincarnated, for a final and supreme effort, the old fierce warrior spirit which had made the tribe of Levi a synonym in earlier times for faithfulness and devotion. But now, alas!

As for the people at large, even the Pharisees, once the Puritans of the race, and who still stood as the chief representatives of the law and as its strictest observers, bowed down and smiled, if only "from the teeth outward," before the foreign power and the "abomination of desolation standing in the holy place." Is not this why John called them afterwards a generation of vipers, their showing such a supple subserviency toward those whom they hated with a venomous hatred?

Over against this degradation of the nation's political and religious life, there rose in the mind of the prophet the sublime ideal of the kingdom of Jehovah. His imagination pictured what it ought to be, what it might be among a faithful people. The histories he meditated showed what it had been aforetime, how blessing had flowed as milk and honey when the nation realised its God, and how His anger had fallen on them in the long seasons of defection. But he felt that all the best must come again,—nay, was he not expressly chosen and appointed to herald it?

Whenever we might conclude the song of Zacharias to have been written, there is no doubt that it expresses the prevailing Messianic hope of the time. Jehovah, the God of Israel, was about to "remember His holy covenant, the oath which He sware to Abraham," "to deliver them out of the hand of their enemies, that they might serve Him without fear, in holiness and righteousness all their days." "The dayspring from on high shall visit us, to shine upon them that sit in darkness and the shadow of death ; to guide our feet into the way of peace." While as for John, he should "be called the prophet of the Highest, go before the face of the Lord to make ready His ways, to give knowledge of salvation unto His people by the remission of their sins." And over this hope and this vocation long and earnestly brooded the soul of John in the wilderness, until the fulness of its meaning and the nearness of its coming stood clear before him.

But the prophet is more than a seer : he is a see-er *plus* the "forth-speaker" of what he sees. "The word of God came to John, the son of Zacharias, in the wilderness. . . . And he came preaching." How did the word of the Lord come? It had also come to other prophets. There is no need to require the audible voice of God : it means that the soul of the prophet became so filled with the divine truth he studied, and a sense of its importance to the people, that his heart was "burdened" with it ; he *must* declare it ; he is "straitened till it be accomplished" ; nay, "woe is to him if he does not preach" it. The streams from the hills of divine truth and rapt contemplation have gradually filled his soul, like some great reservoir, till at length it becomes imperative to provide an outlet. And, seeking God's direction, he is shown the how and when and where.

Whenever we read that the "word of the Lord *came*" to any prophet, we find that soon after, and in consequence of its coming, there is the authoritative proclamation of some truth needful to the times. No purpose could be served by the revealing without the declaring. The "coming" of the word— the λόγος, the doctrine, the inner truth to be uttered—marks the "psychological moment" for the prophet. Seeing has become prophecy ; meditation a message ; the molten truth issues in white-hot words.

CHAPTER IV

"The Word that Burns"

At last "heaven saw the hour ripe on earth." The long silence of the desert was broken by a ringing call of no uncertain sound, the call of one sure of his message, and burning to deliver it.

We can see the tall gaunt figure of the roughly-clad recluse entering one of the scattered hamlets of the borderland, standing like an apparition as he cried out the short, sharp sentence which pierced each of its quiet homes, and penetrated every heart that heard it—"Repent! the kingdom of heaven is at hand!" We can see the groups of people too, children in the foreground, flocking round him wonderingly. To them he is a new embodiment of the law and the prophets. His "Repent!" is an appeal to the former, a demand for a moral "baring" until the bed-rock is reached upon which Jehovah can build; while his statement that "the kingdom of heaven is at hand" is a re-affirmation of old and cherished prophecies.

To the next village he goes, where a similar scene is enacted; and so on, along the hill-slopes and through the valleys, trending toward the Jordan, until at length the whole country side is in a ferment about the new prophet with the old message. He seemed as one of the prophets come to life again—those heroes of an heroic age, who loomed large through the mist of the centuries. His fame soon reached the capital, and Jerusalem, and all Judea, and the region round about Jordan, came out, like the waters of a flood, seeking him.

"It is Elijah come to earth again! The chariot of fire has brought back the prophet who was taken up alive into heaven!" The last note of the old covenant was a promise. And it sounded like a bell through the silent four hundred years with "one clear call" for them: "Behold, I will send you Elijah the prophet before the great and terrible day of the Lord come."[1] Upon this the scribes had taught, and the people believed, that Elijah had to re-appear in bodily presence to proclaim the kingdom and prepare its way.

The points of similarity between the two men were so striking, that it was natural, nay almost unavoidable, that the prophet of the desert should be, in their imagination and belief, "he who should come." Everything about him suggested the old prophet who had not died, who might therefore return at any moment, who *would*, when Jehovah saw fit to send him. With the same startling suddenness had he burst upon the people; there was the same ignorance respecting his former life and training; both appeared among the people as if placed down there by the hand of Jehovah without previous note or warning; the carriage of both was equally fearless, and their message equally uncompromising; and as Elijah had been the right hand of the Almighty as the rebuker of the evils of his time, and in pulling round the nation, by the sheer strength of single-handed faith, to the allegiance from which it had wandered, so the words of the new prophet struck the same high note of demand, and his bearing promised a similar result.

Along the walls of the Hebrew national portrait gallery there hung no picture before which the reverent gazers stopped in admiration at his doing and daring, so instinctively as before Elijah's. Others might represent wisdom or piety or zeal; but his stood for that which strikes an answering chord in every heart—courage. Nor was it to be always a portrait; once again it would descend, take the form of life, and become the same powerful personality as before, to usher in "the notable day of the Lord."

[1] Mal. iv. 5.

When, therefore, they heard the voice of John, and looked upon him, the portrait in their imagination became a living reality before them. And their conclusion was only dispelled, and that not completely, by the direct disclaimer of the prophet—"I am not he."

Disappointed, they ask, "Who art thou, then?" And John's answer is as if he had said: "Do not think of me, or put any weight upon me, at all: who I am matters little or nothing, the kingdom and the King must be supreme with you. I am only a voice. The Eternal is on a progress through His dominions, and I am but the herald who runs before His chariot, crying, "Prepare His way."[1] The *avant-courrier* is only a function—look beyond him to the coming King—"He is mightier than I, the latchet of His sandals I am not worthy to stoop down and untie. Repent! the kingdom of heaven is coming! it is at hand!"

This is, in brief, the significance of John's startling message, and we can readily understand that a fever of excitement and expectation should be produced by it.

The content of the idea of the kingdom of heaven and its King is so totally different to us from what it was to John's contemporaries, that it is only by the aid of the historic imagination that we can in any way understand the force with which it appealed to them, and the effects which it produced. To us the phrase "kingdom of heaven" comes freed from an earthly basis altogether; it is eminently and entirely a spiritual conception. Even so early as the days of the Apostle Paul the spiritual content was pushing out the worldly—"The kingdom of God is righteousness, peace, and joy in the Holy Ghost." And whenever we think of it, it is

---

[1] "The voice of one crying in the wilderness." "Probably 'in the wilderness' should be attached *to the words uttered by the voice*, as is required by the parallelism of Hebrew poetry—

'Prepare ye in the wilderness a way for Jehovah,
Nay, even in the desert a highway for our God.'

The wilderness is metaphorically the barren waste of the Jewish life in that day (Isa. xxxv. 1)."—Farrar on Luke iii. 4.

in a similar light; as established in the affection, the will, the conscience of men; as casting out the evil *there*, and producing *there* loyalty to God. And the kingdom spreads by spreading thus. In a word, with us the connotation of the phrase is ethical, and ethical only.

But what was the meaning of the phrase to those to whom John proclaimed it, and to John himself (for his doubting message to Jesus from the prison conclusively shows that he partook of the popular conception of "the kingdom")? If we were to say that it meant the setting up of a throne in Jerusalem; the founding of an earthly state; the "armies of the Lord" going out to battle and driving the hated Roman domination out of the land; the re-establishment of their nation and city in all the glory that it had in the palmiest days of King David or King Solomon, we should be right, so far. It was just because Jesus, afterwards, while claiming the title of king, was not *such* a king, that the Jews, who, led by the Chief Priests and Scribes, would have followed Him to a man if he had taken such steps as these to justify His title, procured His crucifixion by a mean misrepresentation, to the very power they hated. "We have no king but Cæsar"; "If thou let this man go, thou art not Cæsar's friend!" shouted the hypocrites in their mock loyalty. Representing Him as dangerous to the Roman authority by His use of the title "The King of the Jews," the chief indictment in their minds and hearts was, that He was not dangerous at all.

Still, if we limited the idea of the phrase in the devout Jewish mind to this, we should "do it wrong, being so majestical." It did mean this, but it meant far more than this. Below, above, and around it, was the belief in the overlordship of Jehovah,—in that it lived and moved and had its being. Its first fact was the theocracy; it was ever regarded, by all thoughtful minds and understanding hearts, as having a divine and spiritual foundation.

The ideal began with the beginning of their race, in the call of Abraham to go out and find the place that God should tell him of. And Jehovah promised to make him a great nation. It continued, with ebbings and flowings, it is true, according to the vicissitudes of their history,—but it continued ; never wholly lost, even in the darkest periods, but never fully realised, even in the brightest. Ever after the father of the faithful, God was regarded as the director of the nation's concerns and the giver of its laws. The people were under His control and guidance when but a family. In each development of their tribal and afterwards their national life, the reference was to Him. Moses gave them laws written with His finger ; they were an elect race, a holy nation, a people for God's own possession ; chosen and ordained to conserve His truth, and to maintain, in the midst of a world that wandered from Him, the truths of the unity and spirituality of His nature, and the right He had to reign.

The request of the people for a king was regarded by the prophets and the ardently religious as treason against the Almighty, because it seemed to invade His headship. At length it was granted, but, though a step downwards had been taken, they still believed Jehovah to be behind their king, and ruling through him. Under the bad kings there came a contraction of this belief, or rather the whole belief seemed to be rapidly travelling along the line toward the vanishing point. But Jehovah did not leave Himself without witness. The prophets stood by the law that was losing its sanctions, and the God whose very presence and power seemed to be withdrawing themselves. And "the man who rose to eminence in the commonwealth was the man who had a stronger sense than others in the presence, power, and justice of the invisible King ; and his great function was to awaken the same sense in others by eloquent words and decided acts."[1]

But the course of history was against them. Instead of advancing nearer their ideal, each succeeding age found them apparently farther from it, until, after terrible oppressions and captivities, the colossal power of Rome put down its foot upon their beloved land ; a power that had no "heart of mercy," but

[1] *Ecce Homo.*

pitilessly crushed every insurrectionary aspiration and its leaders. And, further, though it might affect them as a people but to a small extent, yet the whole tendency of the world's thought was away from them, toward perhaps more philosophical, but certainly laxer, religious ideals.

Through all, the people looked for a restitution of Jehovah's kingdom upon earth. It was a dream of the future, based upon that golden age of the past when, under David and Solomon, the nation was in power and splendour; but it was to be infinitely more glorious. This ideal they had kept before themselves alike through temporary success and prolonged oppression. In every day of hope, at every slight favourable turn of affairs, they had eagerly imagined it coming, and through the long night of their disappointment the vision had assumed a magnitude and brightness greater by reason of the darkness that threw it into contrast. But one by one these "gorgeous palaces and cloud-capped towers" had been shattered by the unsparing hand of hard reality. And yet the vision, broken though it might be, burned in the hearts of the people still. Hope deferred maketh the heart sick; yet, sick as it was, the Jewish heart clung to and cherished the hope. Ever did the Hebrews show a remarkable upspringing of belief and hope in the very presence of disaster and defeat.[1]

[1] "A gigantic dream haunted for centuries the Jewish people, constantly renewing its youth in its decrepitude. A stranger to the theory of individual recompense, which Greece diffused under the name of the immortality of the soul, Judea concentrated all its power and love and desire upon the national future. She thought she possessed promises of a boundless future; and as the bitter reality, from the ninth century before our era, gave more and more the dominion of the world to physical force, and brutally crushed these aspirations, she took refuge in the union of the most impossible ideas, and attempted the strangest gyrations. Before the captivity, when all the earthly hopes of the nation had become weakened by the separation of the northern tribes, they dreamt of the restoration of the house of David, the reconciliation of the two divisions of the people, and the triumph of theocracy, and the worship of Jehovah over idolatry. At the epoch of the captivity, a poet (Isaiah), full of harmony, saw the splendour of a future Jerusalem, of which the peoples and the distant isles should be tributaries, under colours so charming, that

It was to this slumbering instinct and smouldering fire that John appealed when his trumpet call woke the desert. The people rose; their long, silent heart-solitude, like that of the wilderness, was broken too. Their heart leaped to the hope, as steel leaps to a powerful magnet. The vision again brightened; patriotic zeal, religious fervour, and moral strength, came to the front, answering the call; and many began to pledge themselves to its realisation. The kingdom of heaven was energised, filled with new forces, vital with that vitality that absorbs and incorporates; and men of energy, who were roused to a profound sense of its importance, seized upon it.[1] Here was the force of the call, "Repent." It was as if John had said: "Bring round your mind from earthly things to this—the coming kingdom; get back to first principles; realise the sanctity of the law, and the unchangeable purpose of Jehovah respecting you as a people. The God who has been over all your history is over you still; He will establish the theocracy once more. Make ye ready the way of the Lord. The chariot of His accomplishing purpose is coming; it is but just over the hill; it holds the King! Smooth, make level the road; fill up the valleys, bring down the mountains; the righteous Jehovah must have a straight path. He is coming, and all flesh shall see His salvation!"

And can we not readily understand how such a message, spoken with no quaver in the voice, but with the confidence of absolute conviction; by one who had "seen the King in His beauty" and talked with Him; from whose presence he had just come; who heralded His advance, and bore His commission, should rouse the people in its tocsin-like appeal? one might say a glimpse of the visions of Jesus had reached him at a distance of six centuries."—*Renan.*

[1] 'Ἀπὸ δὲ τῶν ἡμερῶν Ἰωάννου τοῦ βαπτιστοῦ ἕως ἄρτι ἡ βασιλεία τῶν οὐρανῶν βιάζεται, καὶ βιασταὶ ἁρπάζουσιν αὐτήν."—Matt. xi. 12. The late Dr. Samuel Cox, in *The Expositor*, First Series, vol. iii., suggested the translation of the latter part of this verse which has been adopted in the text: "From the days of John the Baptist until now the kingdom of heaven is energised, and the energetic seize it by force," or "puts forth force, and men of force strongly lay hold upon it.'

For it touched at once the deepest springs of their faith and their highest hopes. No wonder, then, that "Jerusalem, and all Judea, and the region round about Jordan," should turn out their multitudes to see and hear the new prophet.

CHAPTER V

"THE WRATH TO COME."

THE leading religious parties soon heard of the prophet and his preaching; and among the crowds which flocked to the banks of the Jordan came groups of Pharisees and Sadducees. By their distinctive dress, their separateness from the multitude among whom they slowly moved; by the superiority of their demeanour, and that air of refinement that only can come from culture, although the culture may be narrow both in base and superstructure, the penetrative eye of John singled them out.

As we have seen, John had begun to rouse the people from their long lethargy; the bold statement that the kingdom of heaven was at hand had awakened those feelings and hopes which, though they had lain for generations in a trance-like slumber, had never finally died and been buried. And now there appear before him the representatives of those very parties who, professedly and *ex officio*, were above all others seeking the coming of the kingdom and labouring to bring it in; and yet who, in reality, were the greatest obstacles in its way.

And that in two directions. First, by having "the spirit in the letter lost, the substance in the shade." There was every care for the forms of religion, but very little for the spirit; they tithed mint, anise, and cummin, but neglected the weightier matters of the law,—judgment, mercy, and faith. Religion, with one of the parties, had become a careful and anxious round of performing an endless series of absurdly wire-drawn observances, or of the study of equally absurd and wire-drawn commentaries on the sacred text; with the other, it had come to be merely rationalistic morality, from which the supernatural was excluded; while Messiah's coming, or divine intervention, or angel, or spirit, were so many idle tales. The second was, that both of them, one by its supercilious, over-much righteousness, the other by its total indifference, contributed the opiates which prolonged the coma of the nation toward the kingdom and its king.

And John knew that these men, in their venomous pride, spoke with despising of "the common people" who "knew not the law"; that they were men who would resent any infringement of their ecclesiastical position with a calm and assured condemnation in the tone of their question, "By what authority doest thou these things, and who gave thee that authority?" and that, in point of fact, they were men who manipulated the sacred ordinances of religion for the sake of worldly gain, caring most for the social position they conferred—"the chief places in the synagogues and the uppermost rooms at feasts"; while, at the same time, it held good against them, that they lowered themselves and crept at the feet of that civil power which oppressed them, and which they hated. Here was a hypocrisy which included Pharisees and Sadducees both, for if they believed the beliefs they professed to believe, they were manifestly untrue to them in conduct. Must not John, then, have long regarded them in his desert meditations as the greatest hindrances to the re-establishment of the theocracy, with all the benefit and blessing that implied?

Like the Master who came after him, no terms are too hot and scathing for them. "O offspring of vipers,—O viperous brood, who hath warned you to flee from the coming wrath?"[1] "It was bitterly, it was uncourtly,—but oh, it was truly said! They *were* the offspring of vipers, for often had their fathers stung to death

---

[1] Luke (iii.) says it was to "the multitudes" John thus spake, but Matthew reports it as having been addressed to the Pharisees and Sadducees. The latter is much more probable. For Luke has an evident antithesis in ver. 10: "And *the multitudes* asked him, saying, What then shall *we* do?" And further, the description of vipers, dry trees, and chaff is much more appropriate to these special classes than to the people at large.

the benefactors, the saviours, sent from heaven to save the nation ; and soon were the children to show themselves born in the likeness of their sires, by stinging with persecution and death that greater One whose shoe-latchet he was not worthy to unloose."[1]

But in their self-security of righteousness or shallow morality, the Pharisees and Sadducees before the prophet must themselves have been stung by the calm and implied assurance in the question of John that they were obnoxious to, and in the way of, the coming wrath. On the other hand, they expected, as favourites of heaven, to hold high positions among the officers of the kingdom when it should come. But now they are told they are so bad and worthless that they must be swept away by Jehovah's anger before that kingdom can come at all.

To obtain any adequate conception of the force with which these words struck the parties to whom they were addressed, we must ask and try to answer—What was the meaning of the phrase "wrath to come"?

And we must ever keep before our minds the fact that the basal idea of the kingdom of God was not material prosperity or national aggrandisement. These were parts of its superstructure, it is true, but the foundation was purely moral—Jehovah's righteousness. The prophets were always true to spiritual ideals.

One essential factor in the conception was that God would take vengeance on the wicked, and so clear the ground for the establishment of His reign. The "nations may rage, and the kings set themselves, and the rulers take counsel against the Lord and against His Anointed," but "He shall break them with a rod of iron, and dash them in pieces like a potter's vessel."[2] "Jehovah will come with fire, and with His chariots like a whirlwind, to render His anger with fury, and His rebuke with flames of fire. For by fire and by sword will the Lord plead with all flesh ; and the slain of the Lord shall be many."[3] Before Jehovah's house can be filled with His glory, He will "shake the

[1] Ed. Irving.   [2] Ps. ii.   [3] Isa. lxvi. 15, 16.

heavens, the earth, the sea, the dry land, and all the nations."[1] "Jehovah is God in truth ; He is the living God, and an everlasting King : at His wrath the earth trembleth, and the nations are not able to abide His indignation."[2] "He will overthrow the throne of kingdoms, and destroy the strength of the kingdoms of the heathen."[3] These kingdoms are often mentioned by name, and the "burden" proclaimed respecting them,— as Assyria, Babylon, Chaldea, Moab, Ammon, Tyre and Sidon. The nations who oppose the Eternal, and by their evil stand in His way, shall be turned into Sheol, or be so broken that they shall have no power to oppress any more, and His chosen people shall have a free course to run and be glorified.

But not only were outside nations to be rendered powerless by the judgments of Jehovah. Ever true to the ideal of righteousness, the prophets declared that a similar cleansing process must go on inside the elect nation itself: the bad had to be cast out, and the people to be made "all righteous." No privilege of blood or religion can over-ride the moral requirement. In this light consider the opening chapter of Isaiah, where he writes of the vision he saw "concerning *Judah* and *Jerusalem*." How powerful is his indictment, how graphic his picture of their moral delinquency and spiritual degradation ! They are a "sinful nation, a people laden with iniquity, a seed of evil-doers, children that deal corruptly." "The whole head is sick, and the whole heart faint. From the sole of the foot even unto the head there is no soundness in it ; but wounds, and bruises, and festering sores." "Thy silver is become dross, and thy wine mixed with water."

But the Lord shall "turn His hand upon" them, "and throughly purge away the dross," and take away all the "alloy." He will "ease Him of His adversaries, and avenge Himself on His enemies." "The destruction of the transgressors and the sinners shall be together, and they that forsake the Lord shall be consumed."

If there are those, says the same prophet in another place, who

[1] Hag. ii. 6.   [2] Jer. x. 10.   [3] Hag. ii. 22.

have made lies their refuge, and under falsehood have hid themselves, the hail shall sweep away the refuge of lies, and the waters shall overflow the hiding-place.

When "the day" cometh, it shall, says Malachi, "burn as a furnace; and the proud, and all that work wickedness, shall be stubble, and the day that cometh shall burn them up, saith the Lord of Hosts, that it shall leave them neither root nor branch." Zephaniah proclaims that Jehovah will "search Jerusalem with lamps," that "the great day of the Lord is near, it is near and hasteth greatly." "That day is a day of wrath, a day of trouble and distress, a day of wasteness and desolation, a day of darkness and gloominess, a day of clouds and thick darkness, a day of the trumpet and alarm against the fenced cities, and against the high battlements." And through all the prophets it is very clear that Jehovah's judgments begin at His own house.

Neither do the official and privileged classes escape the test of the plummet-line of righteousness because of their position. Jehovah is no respecter of persons. He requires truth in the inward parts. If "prophets prophesy falsely, and priests bear rule by their means," it is in Jehovah's sight "a wicked and a horrible thing."[1] "Woe" is denounced upon the pastors that destroy and scatter the sheep of Jehovah's pasture. It is fearfully possible that the "pastors" may "become brutish, and their flocks be scattered."[2] "Woe be to the shepherds of Israel that do feed themselves! should not the shepherds feed the flocks? Ye eat the fat, and ye clothe you with the wool, ye kill them that are fed, but ye feed not the flock." Zephaniah continues the "woe" upon princes who are roaring lions, judges who are evening wolves, prophets who are light and treacherous persons, and priests who have polluted the sanctuary and done violence to the law.[3] Quotations need not be further multiplied. Enough have been given to illustrate the fact that "the righteous Jehovah loveth righteousness," and that evil will be punished.

[1] Isa. v. 30, 31.   [2] Jer. x. 21; Ezek. xxxiv. 3 *et seq.*
[3] Zeph. iii. 3, 4.

The punishment of the nation, however, severe as it was, was not vindictive. Its purpose was purification. When Jehovah appeareth, He will be like "a refiner's fire, and like fullers' soap; and He shall sit as a refiner and purifier of silver, and He shall purify the sons of Levi, and purge them as gold and silver, and they shall offer unto the Lord offerings in righteousness."[1] Jehovah is more concerned for purity in those who are His than for numbers of adherents who lack that purity. He is not afraid of the pruning-knife, or of committing the great and weighty affairs of His kingdom to "the remnant." The people may be decimated by captivity; cut down as a tree till but the stump is left, but even then "a Branch shall grow out of his roots." "The Lord is mindful of His own." And with the small handful of faithful followers He will begin to reconstruct the kingdom that is to be universal and everlasting.

It may be objected that much of this promise and threatening refers to their national history, and has no larger outlook. And it must be conceded that the idea of the coming kingdom was very composite, and that, moreover, its composition gradually altered as the years and generations came and went, bringing with them and then leaving behind new events and developments. Besides, the continual postponement of its realisation led to its modification. Vengeance was threatened against the nations for their oppression of the chosen people; the judgment was visited; but still the kingdom did not come. "All things continued as they had been from the beginning." Its advent must be put a stage further forward: something else is seen to be an obstacle, let but that be removed, and it will arrive. Time and the course of events removed that, and yet Jehovah delayed His coming. In this the Jewish people were like a party of travellers ascending a renowned but untraversed mountain range. The peak that projects into the heavens far above them seems to be the very summit, but, on arriving there, another and distant peak projects higher still. Weary but patient, they begin to travel the long

[1] Mal. iii. 2, 3.

distance, over broken and disheartening ground, and when at last they arrive at what they fondly hoped was the end of their journey, another and yet more distant summit shows them another and almost hopeless task. And this is repeated until it feels like crossing a continent.

But the very postponement enhanced the people's conception of the glory and beauty of the kingdom when it should arrive, just as the distant mountain peaks we have been imagining seemed more attractive and more magnificent under the bright and alluring light than the stern, rocky reality of present surroundings. And gradually the spiritual interpenetrated itself into the ideal, diminishing the proportion of the material.[1] Thus it was a varied and a changing hope, lacking crispness of conception, slow in its growth, and made up of many parts.

But the element in the conception that remained an invariable factor in all its variations was, that "Jehovah's day" should be ushered in by judgment on all the wicked, inside and outside the nation; it would be "a day of darkness and gloominess, a day of clouds and thick darkness."

As we have seen, the mind of John the Baptist leaned much more to judgment than to mercy. To him that day of wrath was lurid, and its advent close at hand. And there are coming to him the Pharisees and Sadducees, who "neither enter in themselves, nor suffer those who are entering, to go in." At the sight of them his whole soul rises in indignation. How surprised they must have been at the warmth of their reception! and especially so to find that, according to the prophet, they were between

"The full-incensed points of mighty opposites,"

and that neither their smug self-satisfaction nor their ecclesiastical inertia can abide "the day of Jehovah's wrath, nor stand when He appeareth."

"Bring forth fruits meet for repentance"—fruits that correspond

[1] It is most interesting to trace this process through the books of the prophets and the early days of Christianity, until it becomes etherealised, by becoming spiritualised, in the later Epistles of St. Paul.

to and evidence contrition of soul and change of heart, if ye would escape "the coming wrath." It is as if the prophet had said : Before there can be any entrance into the kingdom, you must cease to rely upon multiplied observances or position, and get back to the sweet simplicities and healthy morality of "the first works." "Wash you, make you clean ; put away the evil of your doings from before Jehovah's eyes ; cease to do evil; learn to do well ; seek judgment, relieve the oppressed, judge the fatherless, plead for the widow."

Would they fall back upon the fact that they were Abraham's children, and therefore God's wrath must pass them by? That plea will not stand. The pride and boast of the Jew was his line of descent from "the father of the faithful." And it was to the Hebrews like charity ; it had to cover a multitude of sins. "They could scarcely believe it possible that any son of Abraham should ever be lost."[1] It was the one fact to which they ever harked back, that justified their actions, settled all disputes, put the fullstop to controversy ; the high unscaleable wall behind which they were ever safe, however proud in spirit, superficial in devotion, or heartless and oppressive in conduct.

In boldly taking up the position he did in relation to hereditary privilege, John again allied himself with the prophets. Their royal bard had long before discerned and taught that, before God, blood counted for little and character for much ; the "true generation of them who seek Jehovah's face" are they who have "clean hands and pure hearts, who have not lifted up their souls to vain things, nor sworn deceitfully."[2] "Trust not in lying words, saying, The temple of the Lord, the temple of the Lord, the temple of the Lord, are we," said Jeremiah. For if their ways were not amended, judgment executed, the stranger and fatherless and widow left unoppressed, these *were* lying words. Micah calls upon the heads of the house of Jacob, and rulers of the house of Israel, to hear this : "The heads thereof judge for reward, and the priests thereof teach for hire, and the prophets

[1] Farrar.   [2] Ps. xxiv. 4-6.

thereof divine for money: yet will they lean upon the Lord, and say, Is not the Lord in the midst of us? no evil shall come upon us." But because of this, "Zion shall be plowed as a field, and Jerusalem shall become heaps."[1]

And these are but specimens. All through the prophets, physical descent did not bar judgment when conduct and life were bad. And the strong, swinging arm of John ruthlessly sweeps aside such a refuge of falsehood. The true line of descent is spiritual, inherent in faith and works like those of Abraham. "If the physical were all, Jehovah can raise up children to Abraham of these very stones," said John, pointing to the rough boulders about his feet.

One emblem of barrenness is quickly succeeded by another. They are fruitless trees, nothing coming from them for the glory of God or the betterment of their fellows,—absorbers, yet non-producers. They must be cut down in the day of wrath; and already the gleaming axe lies at their root, the woodman stands by preparing to use it, and there is no one to say, "Woodman, spare that tree," "let it alone another year."[2] And yet they considered themselves to be trees planted by the rivers of water, whose leaf did not wither, and whatsoever they did had Jehovah's blessing, and prospered.

With the doom of fire still present to his thought, he likens them again to the chaff winnowed from the good wheat by the self-elective fan of the greater than himself who was coming after him. Light of character, with little spiritual earnestness or moral

---

[1] Micah iii. 11, 12.
[2] The note of Dr. Farrar on Luke iii. 9 (Cambridge Bible) contains a characteristically beautiful idea. "The notion," says he, "is that of a woodman touching a tree with the edge of the axe to measure his blow before he fells it." But the notion is not self-suggested by the text, and the verb employed seems fatal to it. It is κεῖται (κεῖμαι), "to be laid"; and this, its radical meaning, enters into the varieties of its application. It contains a passive idea. Another verb would be more suitable if he had the axe in his hand. Wesley's note on Matt. iii. 10 is preferable. "The comparison seems to be taken from a woodman who has laid down his axe, to put off his coat, and then immediately goes to work to cut down the tree."

worth, they have no weight to withstand the fan that shall throughly purge the threshing-floor in that day.

How thoroughly roused must the Pharisees and Scribes have felt at the fierce onslaught of the prophet, with such weapons in his hands as vipers, chaff, stones, barren trees!

CHAPTER VI

"WHAT THEN MUST *WE* DO?"

WHILE John has been anathematising Pharisees and Sadducees, various questions have been rising in various minds as to the bearing of the kingdom upon themselves, and what manner of men they ought to be to enter into it. Did they also come under the lash? "And the multitudes asked him, saying, What then must *we* do?" John's answer is plain, direct, and pointed: "He that hath two coats, let him impart to him that hath none; and he that hath food, let him do likewise."

But the question is not the general one it seems at first sight to be; nor is the answer, concrete as it is, such as would only redeem him, though it would do that completely, from the charge of being an unpractical visionary. Both question and answer are specific, and have direct reference to "the kingdom," which formed the "burden" of the preaching of John, and with which he had strongly impregnated the mind of his hearers. It is as if they had said: "What then are we to do to enter it?" And to this John's answer is directed. Those commentators who regard the prophet's reply as simply enjoining general philanthropy have touched the shaft of the arrow, but not its point.

These practical and brotherly kindnesses were to form one of the special and distinguishing marks of the citizens of the kingdom when it should be established. Within a short time after this, Jesus assumed the position of Messiah, and His teaching on this subject proceeds upon these lines. To the disciples who came round Him on "the mountain" in Galilee, Jesus said: "Give to him that asketh thee, and from him that would borrow of thee turn not thou away." When the young ruler came with his earnest and sincere question, he was told to sell all that he had and give it to the poor, and he should have treasure in heaven. And having watched him go away sorrowful, unable to make "the great renunciation," Jesus turned to His disciples with the remarks : " It is hard for a rich man to enter into the kingdom of heaven. Again I say unto you, It is easier for a camel to go through a needle's eye, than for a rich man to enter into the kingdom of God."[1] And if we ask why it was so hard for rich men, the answer is, Because it was to be a law of the Messianic reign that there must be a mutual distribution of goods.

In the great dramatic picture of the Son of Man sitting upon the throne of His glory, Jesus represents Him as judging the nations gathered before Him, and, assisted by all the angels, separating them one from another, as a shepherd divideth the sheep from the goats. The reason why the King shall say unto them on His right hand, "Come, ye blessed of My Father, inherit the kingdom prepared for you," is just the reason we are considering, —they had distributed to the necessity of their brethren,—" For I was an hungred, and ye gave Me meat : I was thirsty, and ye gave Me drink : I was a stranger, and ye took Me in : naked, and ye clothed Me : I was sick, and ye visited Me : I was in prison, and ye came unto Me." . . . "Inasmuch as ye did it unto one of these My brethren, even these least, ye did it unto Me."[2]

In another place Jesus tells His little flock not to fear, for it is their Father's good pleasure to give them the kingdom ; that, therefore, they are to sell that they have, and give alms ; and that they, having sought first the kingdom, shall have food and raiment added, for the Father who feeds the birds and arrays the lilies will care for them.[3]

It was upon this principle that Judas fell back when he saw the waste, as he thought, of the ointment ; it was not in accordance

[1] Matt. xix. 16, *et seq.*   [2] Matt. xxv. 31, *et seq.*   [3] Luke xii. 22, *et seq.*

with the new social law; "it might have been sold and the money given to the poor": and the covetousness of the man is seen in this, that though he recited the law, he "did not care for the poor," but wanted to have the money.

The possession of the bag, the common fund of the society, indicates the practical communism which was to be the rule of life under the Messiah's reign. In "the regeneration," *i.e.* the regenerated social state, the law would be that the interests of each should be identical with the interests of all, and *vice versa*. There would be a perfect balance between egoism and altruism. And it is interesting to find that this was one of the distinguishing traits of the body of the disciples immediately after the ascension: "All that believed were together, and had all things common ; and they sold their possessions and goods, and parted them to all according as any man had need."[1] And when persecution came, this was still their distinguishing feature : "And not one of them said that aught of the things which he possessed was his own, but they had all things common." . . . "As many as were possessors of houses or lands sold them, and brought the prices of the things that were sold, and laid them at the apostles' feet ; and distribution was made unto each, according as any one had need."[2]

To its earliest adherents, the conception of the Christian Church had by no means the same content it has to ourselves ; to them it was the beginning of the realisation of the long-promised kingdom, and shortly Jesus would come back to reign as Messiah. Its communism was, therefore, in accordance with the social duties which would become universal under his reign.

St. Paul exhorts the Corinthians to the same disposition : " For I say not this that others may be eased, and ye distressed ; but . . . that there may be equality : as it is written, He that gathered much had nothing over ; and he that gathered little had no lack."[3] And this he enforces by the example of "the Lord Jesus Christ, who, though He was rich, for their sakes He

[1] Acts ii. 44, 45. [2] *Ibid.* iv. 32, *et seq.* [3] 2 Cor. viii. 13-15.

became poor, that they through His poverty might become rich." And were we to examine all the New Testament references to duty in relation to the poor, it would be found that their force is derived, not from the general feeling of the brotherhood of the race,—after ages spiritualised them into that,—but by their direct relation to the Messianic kingdom.

This social duty of kindly helpfulness to the poor had been of course recognised within the circle of God's chosen people long before the time of John, as far back indeed as the Mosaic legislation itself, the foundation of all their life; and it was, doubtless, upon this that the unwritten law in the minds of John and Jesus and their contemporaries was founded. "If there be with thee a poor man," wrote the author of Deuteronomy (xv. 7, *et seq.*), "one of thy brethren, within any of thy gates in thy land which the Lord thy God giveth thee, thou shalt not harden thine heart, nor shut thine hand from thy poor brother: but thou shalt surely open thine hand unto him, and shalt surely lend him sufficient for his need." And in Leviticus also we read (xxv. 35, *et seq.*): "And if thy brother be waxen poor, and his hand fail with thee; then thou shalt uphold him. . . . Take thou no usury of him, or increase: but fear thy God; that thy brother may live with thee." Much of this chapter is concerned with the affairs of the poor, and the duties of others in relation thereto.

When Isaiah expounds the fast which shall be acceptable to the Lord (lviii. 7, 8), he asks: "Is it not," among other things, "to deal thy bread to the hungry, and that thou bring the poor that are cast out to thy house? when thou seest the naked, that thou cover him; and that thou hide not thyself from thine own flesh?" And, according to Ezekiel, the man who is just, and who shall surely live, is the man who, besides observing other duties, "hath given his bread to the hungry, and covered the naked with a garment" (xviii. 7).

Quotations to the same effect might be largely multiplied, but, the meaning being clear and the case proved, to do so is unnecessary, for, although confirmatory, they would not minister much further light. Yet such an extended and detailed examination of all scriptural references would establish and illustrate our position,—that care for the poor was not only one of the social principles of the elect race, but that it was to receive its fullest and most communistic expansion under the reign of the King Messiah.

We therefore find that John's answer to the question, "What then are we to do (to enter in)?" was one, as said above, not merely enjoining a general philanthropy, but specifically recognising and enforcing the well-understood law incumbent on membership in the coming kingdom.

Then the publicans come with their question : "Teacher, what shall *we* do ?"—by no means an idle question, put for the sake of hearing what kind of an answer the prophet will make in reply, but one that had the sincere purpose of entering the kingdom behind it, for they came "to be baptized."

The Roman government had a peculiarly expeditious method of getting in its revenue.[1] Contracts were made with rich capitalists (*publicani*), who paid a certain agreed-upon sum for the privilege of farming the taxes of the districts of the empire, of which Palestine was one. These sublet the taxes to contractors of a lower grade, who in their turn appointed the actual collectors. It is only the latter who find any mention in the New Testament, with the possible exception of Zaccheus, who may have been one of the "middlemen." It was, of course, the aim of all to make as much over and above the sum paid as possible, while the actual collectors could, without fear of detection, exact more than the specified amount, and keep it. Such a system of taxation, while easy and convenient for the government, readily lent itself to all kinds of extortion and bribery, and was, in fact, the most oppressive of all methods of taxation.

The collectors could only be obtained from the lowest orders of the people, and they were hated, with the intensity of a Jew's hatred, as the constant reminders of their subjection to the tyranny of the conqueror ; as traitors to their own people, because

[1] See Smith's *Dictionary of the Bible*, art. Publican.

they had become his tools, and their interest was with him rather than with them ; and because of their extravagant greed. "They were regarded almost with horror, and were always included in the same category with harlots and sinners. When an occupation is thus despised and detested, it is clear that its members are apt to sink to the level at which they are placed by the popular odium."[1] How strong then must have been the preaching of John when it could thus powerfully move this, the lowest class of the population, with its earnestness!

John's reply to their question was "not a summons to temple service or sacrifice, nor was it ascetic or revolutionary in its tone." "Exact," said he, "no more than is appointed you." "Extortion was the fierce temptation of the class. It would have been easier for the publicans to keep all the ritual than radically to change the whole spirit of their lives." "He tested sincerity in a manner at once definite and practical. His answer involved no doctrine of human brotherhood or divine fatherhood ; it was a dogmatic appeal to the conscience of men who had laid their ethical sense to sleep."[2] So they received *their* answer,—one so complete and self-evident that from it there was no appeal.

The helmet crests and the dress, the erecter forms and lighter features of groups of soldiers, move about among the crowds, as they push their way, as soldiers will, to the front. The name given to them (στρατευόμενοι) indicates that they were on active service, and not "off duty" from the Jerusalem or other garrison, who had come to be "in at" the new excitement. But there were no military operations afoot at this time of which we have any knowledge. They were probably on service among these crowds themselves, for the authorities responsible for the public peace were aware of the highly inflammable nature of the Jews, and knew how readily a tumult might arise at the call of the prophet if he were so minded. Indeed, the fear of an insurrectionary outbreak is given by Josephus as the reason of Herod's subsequent arrest of John.

[1] Farrar.   [2] Reynolds.

Apparently careless, but alert, they move about in small groups among the people, and, coming near the prophet, break a lance with him : " And what shall *we* do ? " It is not probable that there was any seriousness in this question ; the soldiers, whether Romans or mercenary, would have no adequate sense, probably no sense at all, of the meaning of the phrase which had so deeply stirred the hearts of the Jewish people about them. The scripture does not say, either, as it does in the case of the publicans, that the purpose of baptism was behind the question. It was put in a light, bantering way ; the questioners were both curious and careless for the answer.

The surprising thing is that the fierce spirit of John did not boil over in scalding words at the power the soldiers represented. Here was the colossal power of Rome, with its iron heel upon the country, its domination hated by all patriots, the chief external hindrance to the kingdom, yet there is no word of denunciation, nor, even when the door is open for it, is there any suggestion of irritation or rebellion. His reply is personal, not national.

The careless soldiers must have been surprised at its pointedness. Its three parts were short, sharp home-thrusts—" Do not extort money by threats or violence from any man." It was not easy for quiet civilians to resist the demands, although unjust, of trained soldiers, strong in physique, and without effeminate pity for those from whom money might be extracted. Mercy, consideration for such had but small weight with them. " Do not cheat by false accusation ; be too honest to act as mere informers ; do not bleed people's purses by threatening to lay fictitious charges." On the other hand, " Be content with your pay, and as you agreed to it, when you went into the service, let it serve you."

These instances are given by the Evangelist, not as exhaustive, but as typical. All sorts and conditions of men came to John, many doubtless sincere in their queries, and others to hear what he would say, how he would meet their difficulties. " And many other things in his exhortation preached he unto the people." This was the style of his preaching. However various the classes of people or the types of character, his "exhortation" took them back to righteousness of conduct, to the first principles of ordinary morality. There was with him no slight and hasty dealing with sin; he required evidences of reform in character, in "good works."

The way, then, to enter into the kingdom of heaven, is, according to the Baptizer, not to let our "inwardness," our μετάνοια, suffice; neither to sit down and see visions and dream dreams, but to engage in those practical humanities of "neighbourliness" which are the evidences of having passed through the strait gate into the narrow way that leadeth unto life.

CHAPTER VII

"The Baptism of John"

"And they were baptized of him in the river Jordan, confessing their sins."

The principal question for us here is—What was the meaning and significance of John's baptism, to the prophet himself and to his disciples? For, just as there is a wide divergence in the idea of the kingdom of heaven between his day and ours, so also there is a great and corresponding difference on this subject. In by far the greater part of Christendom baptism possesses certain doctrinal attachments, of which the authoritative communication of divine and regenerating grace, through the hands of the priest at the time of its administration, is the chief. But these it certainly did not possess to the mind of the Baptizer. Whether these additions or developments can be justified because of the fuller baptism of the Spirit under Christ, and continued to His Church, is a large and important question; but it is not now before us: putting all these things aside, the question for us is— What did this rite mean to John and to those who came to receive it at his hands?

It need hardly be insisted on that the prophet did not originate the ceremony; he found it already in existence, and for purposes and with significance similar to his own. Evidence to almost any required amount exists and is easily accessible, that the rite was in use both among the Jews and many Gentile nations. Lustrations and baptisms of various kinds prevailed throughout the civilised world. The Romans, the Greeks, the dusky peoples of the East, all employed it ; and, as the footnote shows, it was observed by the North American Indians (where did they get the idea ?), and with a beautiful meaning too.[1] So that we need not spend time upon proof or illustration, or upon the controverted method of its administration,—these would prove pleasant "by-path meadows," but we must keep before us the one idea of *John's* baptism.

John, then, adopted a rite already well known, but he attached to it a new purpose and pledge. With him it was a simple and earnest symbolic act. The root-idea of its symbolism is natural, patent, almost self-suggestive. It is the power and suitability of water to take away uncleanness from "the outer man." And everyone in the crowds which assembled day after day on the banks of the Jordan, coming to his baptism, was perfectly familiar with this idea. It had been in their sacred records for generations, and was often heard and read in public worship and exposition, and doubtless in private devotion too. "Wash me throughly from mine iniquity and cleanse me from my sin." "Who shall ascend into the hill of the Lord, or who shall stand in His holy place ? He that hath clean hands and a pure heart." "Wash you, make you clean, put away the evil of your doing from before mine eyes." "I will sprinkle clean water upon you, from all your filthiness and from all your idols will I cleanse you ; a new heart will I give unto you." In all of which we find linked together the external act of purification and its spiritual significance.

[1] "A striking instance of the primitive significance of the symbol is given by Frederika Bremer. A tribe of Indians on the Mississippi, on the first day of the year, assemble and plunge into the river, and rise to begin a new life. This ceremony is called the *Bushkiton*. No quarrel is allowed to survive that act. Should anyone, after that, attempt to rake up a former feud, he is at once reminded that the water of the *Bushkiton* has quenched the last spark of animosity. Should anyone allude to any unworthy act of any member of the tribe which occurred before the ceremony took place, he is silenced at once by the memento, ' He has passed the *Bushkiton*.' Every one reckons himself ' dead indeed unto' all the errors of his past life. He rises from that plunge to ' walk in newness of life.' "—Quoted in Dr. Gregory's *Handbook of Scriptural Church Principles*.

To John and his disciples it meant, then, that those who received it were desirous of leaving, and were resolved to leave, their past sinfulness of life, and to get back, by the divine remission of sins, to those simple, clear, and earnest conditions of heart through which alone God can work for the establishment of His kingdom. In this John is in line with Moses and all the prophets, who were ever faithful to the spiritual basis as the first essential for the coming of the kingdom of God. It therefore expressed contrition for having been negligent of the existence and claim of the divine kingdom, and for harbouring that personal evil which denied God's rule and obstructed its advent; for having been content with the state of things around them, and drifting farther and farther from its realisation. But baptism was the burial service of the old nature and course of life. It was a re-pentance, a change of mind, heart, and purpose, the first condition of that remission of sins which was to fit them for being the agents of the kingdom,—a coming back in thought, affection, life.

With a special force did the baptism of John appeal to men in whom the religious sense was deep and strong, "men of energy";[1] and separated such from the great mass of their fellow-countrymen. His call was much too severe for the acceptance of those who form so large a part of every community,—those who have "itching ears," and the roots of whose religious life wander weakly about in a thin surface-layer of excited emotion. The chaff could not stand even John's winnowing-fan. While to those who accepted it, baptism stood as the Rubicon between them and their former life,—" the course of this world." Their citizenship henceforth was a heavenly one.

But the baptism of John implied still more. It meant the pledge and dedication of themselves for the bringing in of the kingdom just at hand. They are now instruments in the hand of Jehovah for this purpose, and they will strive to keep that inward

[1] See Dr. Cox and Dr. Bruce's papers on Matt. xi. 12 in *The Expositor*, First Series, vols. iii. and v.

moral state which alone is suitable as the prepared and straightened way of the Lord. They expect its coming, they are going to work for it, they place themselves at its service.

So far and no farther did the baptism of John go. There was no Pentecost in his movement. It was confessedly limited in its scope and meaning. "I indeed baptize you with water; but there cometh He that is mightier than I, the latchet of whose shoes I am not worthy to unloose: He shall baptize you with the Holy Spirit and fire, whose fan is in His hand, throughly to cleanse His threshing-floor, and to gather the wheat into His garner; but the chaff He will burn up with unquenchable fire."[1]

In regard to the interpretation of baptism "with the Holy Spirit and fire," we are not of course to ask "what exposition will it bear?" and answer according to subsequent events and doctrinal developments, but "what did John mean by it, to whom these developments were unknown?" To suppose that *he* looked forward to the day of Pentecost, as the time of its chief fulfilment, would be to attribute to him a foreknowledge he did not possess; while to consider him as conscious of the dogma of the Holy Spirit, as future ages formulated it, and of the spiritualised application of the doctrine of the Spirit's baptism to the "Church throughout all the world," as we have the doctrine to-day, would be to imagine him possessed of a still more impossible prescience. We must again say that John's code of ideas was purely Messianic; he had no outlook beyond the national expectation.

By keeping this in mind, the interpretation of this fine passage is not far to seek, especially if we bring to bear its beautiful parallelism. As we have already seen, one essential part of the conception of the coming of the kingdom was a day of judgment, which should separate the evil and the good. At present the nation is mixed, like the wheat and chaff that lie upon the threshing-floor before the winnowing. The use of the fan will be to divide the mass into those worthy to enter the kingdom— those, *i.e.*, who stand the test, and fall down, of full weight, as the

[1] Luke iii. 16, 17.

good grain falls; and those who, light and worthless according to the divine standard, are the chaff, blown some distance away, where it falls in a loose, irregular heap.

The fan will be the divine breath or wind—the Holy Spirit (τὸ πνεῦμα τὸ ἅγιον). The words here employed are the exact equivalent of the Hebrew words in John's mind; possibly, probably, the words he also used (*ruach Elohim, ruach Jehovah, ruach Kodesh*). The words indicate the divine Spirit as "giving effect to the will of God in the world of matter and mind."[1]

At the very beginning of Scripture we read that when the earth was without form and void, and darkness was upon the face of the deep, the first step in its reduction from chaos to cosmos was that "the Spirit, or breath, of God, moved upon the face of the waters." The Psalmist (Ps. xxxiii. 6) tells us that all the host of heaven were made "by the breath of Jehovah's mouth." Concerning the same subject of the creation, Isaiah asks: "Who hath directed the Spirit of the Lord (still the same word, meaning breath or influence or power), or being His counsellor hath taught Him?" (Isa. xl. 13). In his reasoning with Job (xxxiii. 4), Elihu reminds him that "the Spirit of the Lord hath made him, and the breath of the Almighty hath given him life," evidently referring to the account of the creation of man in Genesis. When the *breath* has breathed upon the slain in the valley of dry bones (Ezek. xxxvii.) and they live, we read: "Thus saith the Lord to the house of Israel (who are the dry bones of the vision), Behold, O My people, and ye shall know that I am Jehovah when I have put My *Spirit* in you." And as both words are the same, the identity of the breath and the Spirit of Jehovah is proved. This Spirit is at once the authority and the inspiration of the prophet: "The Spirit of the Lord God is upon me," says Isaiah (lxi.). And this gave him the commission to preach good tidings unto the poor, to bind up the broken-hearted, to proclaim liberty to the captives, and the opening of the prison to them that were bound.

We need not extend examples, although they would corroborate

[1] Davies, *Hebrew Lexicon*.

the general conclusion ; which is, that the Spirit of Jehovah, or of Elohim, represents the divine energy as effective of its purpose in creation and mind, and in separating men for special work. To John the conception of Jehovah doing His will among the armies of heaven and also among the inhabitants of the earth was a very old one ; and his words to the people before him are but another application of it. The Spirit shall distinguish and divide between the good and bad in Messiah's kingdom.

His is a tentative work and undiscriminating. He will baptize all with water who come to him, unto repentance,—the change of mind and attitude suitable to welcome the day of Jehovah: but He who was coming after him would come with discernment of spirit ; and, baptizing with the divine breath or wind, the chaff would be blown away from the good wheat as effectively as it was done on the summer threshing-floor.

The adjective "holy" indicates that it is peculiarly God's own. "Very conspicuous," says Dr. Beet,[1] "especially in the writings of St. Luke, is the term *Holy Spirit*, already used in the Septuagint as a rendering of the phrase *Spirit of Holiness* in Ps. li. 11 ; Isa. lxiii. 10. The Spirit of God claims the epithet as being in a very special manner the source of an influence of which God is the one and only aim. All other influences tend away from God. He is therefore, in a sense shared by no other inward motive principle, "*The Holy Spirit.*"

Further, it is very manifest that, if the Messianic interpretation of the passage be the only right interpretation, as we contend it is, and if we follow out its fine parallelism, the "fire" is to be applied to the chaff. The Breath separates, the good wheat is gathered into the garner of the kingdom, the chaff is burned up by a fire that is fierce, unquenchable, till all is consumed, as must have been the case if the chaff of the threshing-floor once caught fire.

When Jesus afterward spoke of His kingdom, He sanctioned, if He expanded, the concept of it which his forerunner had pro-

[1] "*Holiness as understood by the Writers of the Bible.*"

pounded. And when he had occasion to speak of judgment in relation thereto, he adopted the ideas of John respecting it. "The kingdom of heaven is like a man who sowed good seed in his field, but his enemy came and sowed tares." Both are to grow together until the harvest, when the reapers will be directed to "gather up the tares, and bind them in bundles to burn them." "The kingdom of heaven is like a drag-net which was cast into the sea, and gathered fish of every kind, which, when it was filled, they drew up on the beach; and they sat down, and gathered the good into vessels, but the bad they cast away. So shall it be in the consummation of the age. The angels shall come forth, and sever the wicked from among the righteous, and shall cast them into the furnace of fire; there shall be the weeping and the gnashing of teeth." It is clear, therefore, that one part of the idea of fire baptism is that of separation and judgment.

But there is in that saying of John we are now considering more than a parallelism. Other thoughts besides those of judgment would be awakened in his own and his hearers' minds by the symbol of fire. Fire was the manifestation of Jehovah to accept and consecrate His people. It was associated with His highest revealings. To John and his audience "it would recall the scene when their father Abraham asked Him who promised that he should inherit the land wherein he was a stranger, Lord, whereby shall I know that I shall inherit it?" The answer came thus. He was standing under the open sky at night, watching by the cloven sacrifices, when, "behold, a smoking furnace and a burning lamp that passed between those pieces." It would recall the fire which Moses saw in the bush, which shone and awed and hallowed even the wilderness, but did not consume; the fire which came in the day of Israel's deliverance, as a light on their way, and continued with them throughout the desert journey; which burned upon the summit of the sacred mountain, and out of which Jehovah spake; "the fire which descended on the tabernacle in the day when it was reared up, and abode upon it continually; which shone in the Shekinah; which touched the lips of Isaiah; which flamed in the visions of Ezekiel; and which was yet again promised to Zion, when the Lord will create upon every dwelling-place upon Mount Zion, and upon all her assemblies, a cloud and smoke by day, and the shining of a flaming fire by night." [1]

As to the individual, the two baptisms—water and fire—hold a contrast within their similarity, the contrast of the external and the internal. When one of the seraphim laid the living coal from off the consecrating altar upon Isaiah's mouth, he said, "Lo, this hath touched thy lips, and thine iniquity is taken away, and thy sin purged." And following on that came the offer of, and the commission to, service. Probably this indicates the highest meaning of the symbolism of fire in the thought of the prophet,—cleansing, consecrating, commissioning, invigorating, for the coming kingdom.

It was with no querulous tones in his voice that he thus defined the limits of his own, and recognised the superiority of his Successor's work. With splendid humility, thorough acceptance of his position, unquestioning loyalty to the divine will that made another greater than himself, he who had spoken of himself as the *avant-courrier* of the King, now declares that he is unworthy to be the most menial bondservant in the household, whose business it is to loose the sandals off the master's feet when he comes home, and wash his feet.

It was because of the subordinate position of the founder of the movement that the movement itself lacked finality. His disciples became scattered abroad in course of time, and probably shadows of deepening disappointment came upon them as the weeks and months passed away, and there were no signs of fulfilment; shadows that fell upon the great soul of the Baptist himself, as we shall see. "It was a solemn scene, doubtless, when crowds from every part of Palestine gathered by the side of the Jordan, and there renewed, as it were, the covenant made between their ancestor and Jehovah. It seemed the beginning of a new age, the re-

[1] Arthur's *Tongue of Fire*, 26th ed. pp. 1, 2.

storation of the ancient theocracy. . . . But many of those who witnessed the scene, and shared in the enthusiasm it awakened, must have remembered it in later days as having inspired hopes which had not been realised."[1]

It was in this condition that St. Paul found "certain disciples" at Ephesus. These had been baptized with John's baptism, but had not so much as heard of the Holy Spirit. And when the apostle showed them how John had directed his disciples to Him who should come after him, they also were baptized in the name of the Lord Jesus. "And when Paul had laid his hands upon them, the Holy Spirit came on them."

While, therefore, within its own limits, John's baptism was "from heaven," yet, upon the other hand, it was but tentative,— professedly so; divinely destined to merge into the divinely permanent.[2]

[1] *Ecce Homo.*
[2] Josephus's testimony to the Baptist is interesting and valuable, although it is manifest that he had not a clear and full idea of the meaning of his baptism. He says that John "was a good man, and commanded the Jews to exercise virtue, both as to righteousness toward one another, and piety toward God, and so to come to baptism; for that the washing (with water) would be acceptable to him, if they made use of it, not in order to the putting away (or the remission) of some sins (only), but for the purification of the body: supposing still that the soul was thoroughly purified beforehand by righteousness."—*Ant.* Bk. xviii. ch. 5.

CHAPTER VIII

"Comest Thou to Me?"

ALL through, the Baptist has been true to his own description of himself as the herald who runs before the chariot, the "voice" that proclaimed its coming. If we ask for the ground of his confident assertion that "there standeth one among you whom ye know not," we have for answer, first, his assured belief in the nearness of the Messiah's approach; and, second, "He that sent me to baptize with water, said unto me, Upon whomsoever thou shalt see the Spirit descending and abiding upon Him, the same is He that baptizeth with the Holy Spirit." In the prophet's mind there hovered this great expectancy. "So I baptize, and watch for the opening heavens; He is among you, He will shortly present Himself, and by that sign be both manifested and recognised."

And now the time had arrived to introduce the King Himself. It would be an error, however, to suppose that John knew Jesus as the Messiah directly he saw Him among the people, or as soon as He became a candidate for his baptism. The Baptist's self-depreciation, "I would need to be baptized of Thee, and comest Thou to me?" was due to another cause, as we shall see. The Kingship of Jesus remained unseen, even by the prophet's piercing eyes, until the heavens opened, and the Spirit descended like a dove and alighted on Him. All he knew was that there was *someone* among them who was divinely destined to the Messiahship, but the individual he did not know. But that he was among them he was certain; it was the very root of his mission; it gave it its meaning and purpose; unless that were so, it would have no *raison d'être* at all. He may possibly have had surmisings, pre-judgments, as to who it might be, but if he had, he felt he had no right to take away the interrogation mark behind them, and state them as conclusions.

Among the crowds that gathered, day after day, thick as swarms of bees, on the river banks, to hear the uncompromising prophet and to receive his baptism, came a young man from Galilee, the cousin of the Baptizer, who at length presented himself. Probably he was personally known to John. It is reasonably certain that "the prophecies which went before on them," when their mothers met, would not be allowed to fall into such abeyance or to be of such little influence, that the cousins did not see each other through all the years of their youth; and although they lived so far apart, one in Galilee and the other in the hill-country of Judea, yet many would be the opportunities of meeting they had in Jerusalem at the celebration of the great religious festivals,—festivals which two such youths would, as a matter of course, attend. John was aware of

"Those sinless years
That breathed beneath the Syrian blue";

of the reputation of Jesus; of His quiet ways and pure life and gentle demeanour; of that insight into the principles and spiritual meaning of the sacred records which, even at twelve years of age, forced Him, to the forgetting of all else, into the presence of the doctors of the law, to hear the learned men of His nation and ask them questions. Of all this John could not well be ignorant. We therefore take the phrase, "I knew Him not," to mean, "I knew Him not as the Messiah."

For years, however, they had not seen each other; on quite different planes had their lives moved. John had dwelt amid the rigours of the desert, Jesus in a quiet village home; John had forsaken the world, Jesus had remained in it and fulfilled its daily duties; John's course for the most part had been one of cataracts and rapids, that of Jesus "in green pastures and beside waters of rest." But, given true hearts, absence and the lapse of time make no difference to appreciation and friendship, except it be to deepen them; and when they met, spirit answered to spirit in a flash of mutual recognition.

When the purpose of Jesus to be baptized became manifest, the Baptist quickly put in an earnest disclaimer: " I have need to be baptized of Thee, and comest Thou to me?—of this honour I am not worthy.' The head which had been carried high bows itself; the voice which had spoken with no softened accents to the brood of vipers, which had been inflexible in propounding practical righteousness, now falls into other and gentler tones, and new and strange acknowledgments. In all probability he had no idea of the divinity of Jesus; he sought to decline the honour, not on supernatural grounds, but upon those of spiritual superiority. He laid the staff of authority down, and bent himself before the greater, doing " obeisance to the royalty of inward happiness." It was the same feeling as that which finds its parallel and illustration in the case of Peter afterwards, when, at the Last Supper, Jesus would have washed his feet. To him the natural order seemed reversed; he would gladly wash the Master's feet, but for the Master to wash his! In utmost surprise does he say, "Thou shalt never wash *my* feet!" To those who knew Him, the personal supremacy of Jesus was ever unquestioned and accorded.

It is instructive to note that Jesus pressed His request for baptism, and overruled the protest of the Baptist: "Suffer it to be so now, for thus it becometh us to fulfil all righteousness." It is as if Jesus had said: " The question of our relative positions or merits is one we will not raise now, both of us want to bring in the kingdom of heaven, which is just at hand; it is befitting that everything which takes practical steps toward its incoming should be observed by us. Your baptism is one of them, it pledges to that righteousness of life which is one of the essentials of the kingdom; so that, allow it to be so now." "Then he suffered Him." Jesus accepted and, by accepting, sanctioned the purpose of the ordinance, just as before He had observed the Temple services, and as afterwards He continued to observe them. He did not over-ride, count lightly, or neglect anything of value under the old covenant; He was "under the law." Generally speaking, we have a dim, ill-defined idea that Jesus need not have obeyed the law unless He wished to, for was He not the Lord of the law? But He Himself said that He "came not to destroy the law, but to fulfil it." Consistently with this, the records of His life show Him as fulfilling it all along the line. It was observed for Him at His birth,—His parents came to offer sacrifice "according to the law of the Lord." And all through His life He acknowledged it. No inconsistencies or failures in respect of it were ever alleged against Him. His enemies followed Him about, lynx-eyed, watching every movement, no peccadillo could have slipped them; but so lawful was His whole career, that even at His trial the capital sentence could only be secured on the evidence of lies that were despicable. Had Jesus ever broken the law, it must have come out then.

And although the Baptist's ordinance was not invested with the authority of a Mosaic enactment, yet Jesus was prepared to sanction and approve everything that made for righteousness. The same attitude re-appeared when John the disciple came to Him and said: "Master, we saw one casting out devils in Thy name, and we forbade him, because he followeth not with us." But Jesus said: "Forbid him not, for there is no man who shall do any mighty work in My name, and be able quickly to speak evil of Me. For he that is not against us is for us."

But besides this personal ground of John's disclaimer, there was another, viz. the nature of his baptism, and its felt inappropriateness to Jesus. We have seen that it was—(1) "Unto remission of sins," and (2) Dedication to sincere endeavour to bring in the kingdom. Whatever may be our opinion as to the incidence of the first of these in the case of Jesus, it is certain that John at least felt his baptism to be beside the mark for Jesus, that He had no need of repentance, that there was nothing in Him to require it or its implied remission of sins, that Jesus was more qualified to enter the kingdom than he was.

The interesting and important question here emerges—Did Jesus, in thus accepting baptism, nay, pressing for it at the hands of John, accept it for *Himself* in its totality of meaning, for it was a βάπτισμα μετανοίας, a baptism of repentance? There are some considerations which lead us to a simple, direct, and natural answer.

The first is, that we have no evidence that Jesus was conscious of His destiny as the Messiah until His baptism. The Gospel histories do not reveal that He had any knowledge of His divine nature, or of His designation, or of the possession of miraculous powers, before this event, while they do consistently show that He possessed and used them all after it. The descent of the Spirit upon Him at that time was the official designation, so to speak, to His life's work; the revelation that indicated the Father's meaning, and filled out, if the expression may be allowed, the soul of Jesus both with knowledge and power. A few sentences comprise all that is told us of His earlier life, and they tell us of development. There was a real sense in which "Jesus advanced in wisdom" as well as "in age, and in favour with God and man"; He "grew and waxed strong, becoming full of wisdom." The account of the scene of Jesus in the Temple among the doctors is often misread. We are not told of the doctors asking questions of Him, waiting for His answers as out of a divine and recondite knowledge; but that the boy of twelve was hearing them, the teachers of the people, and asking them questions, as a youth strong in spirit and desirous to learn; while the doctors on their part were "astonished at His understanding and answers," at His comprehension of the truths and principles of the law. To assume the prescience of Jesus before His baptism, in regard to His nature and Messiahship, is to take up a position which necessitates occult and metaphysical explanations, all of which, it seems to us, are obviated by the simple and scriptural position we take up as to the meaning of the baptism to Jesus Himself.

And this position shows us how Jesus could accept baptism from the hands of John. He came to the bank of the Jordan, attracted by the reputation of the prophet, when, impressed by the importance, forcefulness, and truth of his preaching, He entered the lists for baptism as one of those earnest spirits who eagerly desired the coming of the kingdom, and pledged Himself to help to bring it in. It may seem at first sight as if John's disclaimer, " I have need to be baptized of Thee," implied some such foreknowledge, but we need to separate between this statement, and "There standeth one among you whom ye know not, it is He the latchet of whose shoes I am not worthy to unloose." For John to say the former to Jesus when He came does not imply that he, there and then, recognised Him to be the latter. The disclaimer was upon personal and moral, not upon official, grounds. Besides, we have the prophet's direct statement, that " I knew Him not: but He that sent me to baptize with water, He said unto me, Upon whom thou shalt see the Spirit descending and alighting upon Him, the same is He that baptizeth with the Holy Spirit. And I have seen, and have borne witness that this (Jesus, who was coming towards him) is the Son of God."

The second consideration is, that everyone who accepted baptism at the hands of John accepted it in its general meaning and purpose, and applied it to his own spiritual condition. In fact, he could accept it in no other way. And there must have been a variety of spiritual conditions as great as the individual cases that presented themselves. To some the meaning of the rite would be a strong but diffused desire with vague ideas; to others, material and social progress and national aggrandisement would loom the largest; while to others, again, the spiritual would be the most prominent part of the conception. We cannot reduce all the adherents of new movements to the same unbroken level of spiritual nature or expectation. And many a man who attaches himself to such movements does so accepting the general *motif*, but by no means pledging himself to every tenet and position.

Let us apply this to the case before us. The movement of John necessarily had a large range, but we have no warrant to stretch everyone who accepted its initiatory ceremony to fit it all, from its Alpha to its Omega. We have seen that the baptism of John meant (1) confession of sin, and (2) a pledge to bring in the heavenly kingdom. In Jesus' acceptance there was certainly the acceptance of the latter; yet it would be quite illogical to make it include the former.

The evangelical commentators hold a very strong position in the sinlessness of Jesus. He did no sin, neither was there deceit in His mouth; and neither before nor after the baptism have we any indication of the slightest breath to dull the mirror of His fair fame. And to this position the Baptizer lends his strong support by his instant recognition of spiritual superiority. But, failing to recognise our principle,—*that Jesus accepted baptism only in so far as it applied to Himself*, as "becoming" in the fulfilment of all points of righteousness,—His very sinlessness makes it a greater difficulty for them to interpret the fact of Jesus receiving a baptism, one part of whose meaning was repentance unto remission of sins.

This difficulty was felt in the early Church. A heretical and apocryphal writing, generally included in Cyprian's works, appears to have attributed to Jesus a confession of His own sins at His baptism. Strauss does not, of course, agree with the solution of the difficulty by modern theologians, but he has well defined the dilemma itself. He says [1] that "the sum of what they have contributed toward the removal of the difficulty consists in the application to Jesus of the distinction between what a man is as an individual and what he is as a member of the community. He needed, say they, no repentance on His own behalf, but, aware of its necessity for all other men, the children of Abraham not

[1] *Life of Jesus*, Eng. Trans. vol. i. p. 351.

excepted, He wished to demonstrate His approval of an institution which confirmed this truth, and hence He submitted to it."

The theologians make the baptism part of Jesus' vicarious relation to the world,—expanding its significance by metaphysics until it includes His temptation, and as it cannot include His own sin, then "the sins of the whole world." Dr. Reynolds may stand as the type of this large and influential class of expositors,[1] the more so because of the definiteness of his elucidation and the liberality of his spirit. Summarised in his own words, the case is stated thus: "His submission to this ordinance of confession was a part of that unutterable humiliation by which He brought in and fulfilled the eternal righteousness. He who bore our sins on Calvary confessed their guilt and shame in the Jordan. . . . Confession of sin could not, need not, mean in His case the remembrance and disclosure of a corrupt nature, or the acknowledgment of base motives and unworthy deeds. . . . The Lord took our humanity upon Him. The Son of God felt, through human flesh and creature limitation and temptations to sin, all the curse, the darkness, the perplexities, the humiliations of our fallen race. He was not, and could not be, conscious of personal corruption or defilement, but He must have felt, in a degree in which no other person ever did or could have done, the burden, the curse, the peril, and the shame of SIN ; not of His own sins, but of the sins of the world, the sins of the theocratic kingdom, the sins of those whom His Father had given Him, and of the nature which, in His infinite condescension, He had assumed . . . None could know like the incarnate God what sin was ; none but He has fathomed the need of human nature. He alone estimated fully the regeneration which He declared essential to the formation of His kingdom. If so, who can rival the Lord Jesus in confessing the sins of the whole world?"

We may perhaps add to this, as being in the same line, the exposition of Dean Chadwick :[2] "But here we meet a deeper

---

[1] *John the Baptist*, 2nd ed. p. 321, *et seq.* New York, Barnes & Co.
[2] "The Gospel of St. Mark," *Expositor's Bible.*

question : not why Jesus accepted baptism from an inferior, but why, being sinless, He sought for a baptism of repentance. How is this act consistent with absolute and stainless purity?

"Now it sometimes lightens a difficulty to find that it is not occasional or accidental, but wrought deep into the plan of a consistent work. And the Gospels are consistent in representing the innocence of Jesus as refusing immunity from the consequences of guilt. He was circumcised, and His mother then paid the offering commanded by the law, although both these actions spoke of defilement. In submitting to the likeness of sinful flesh, He submitted to its conditions.... When He tasted death itself, which passed upon all men, for that all have sinned, He carried out to the utmost the same stern rule to which at His baptism he consciously submitted.... Baptism was avoidable, and that without any compromise of His influence, since the Pharisees refused it with impunity, and John would fain have exempted Him. Here, at least, he was not 'entangled in the machinery,' but deliberately turned the wheels upon Himself."

Both these expositions, which may stand as expressing the position of what may be termed the strictly orthodox school, proceed upon the assumption that Jesus was conscious of His divine nature and Messianic destiny *before* His baptism, and that therefore His baptism was part of a pre-arranged plan. But this is a position not only full of metaphysical difficulties, as to how one could possess limited human and unlimited divine knowledge at one and the same time, but is also, as we have intimated, unsupported by scriptural evidence. The circle of Jesus' impeccability is drawn; then from a point far outside it, another is described, whose circumference is made to approach as near as possible, but not quite to touch, that of the former,—the circle of the sin of the world; then its malarial haze is blown over the surface of the former, with the suggestion rather than the statement that that meets all the requirements of the case. But who, reading the Gospel narratives naturally, would spontaneously think of the subtle distinctions and intricacies which this theory necessarily involves. Our contention is, that it was at the baptism Jesus became conscious of His divine nature and Messianic destiny. This is not only the most natural position in itself, but it also lends immense weight and significance to the Temptation, which immediately followed, and gives the strongest of all reasons for Jesus settling and maturing, in the wilderness, that "plan" of life and work from which He never swerved.

All the difficulties are obviated, yet the sinlessness of Jesus is preserved intact, by the adoption of the simple and scriptural exegesis we advocate. To sum up: We hold that our answer to the important question raised by Jesus accepting baptism at the hands of John—(1) That He was not conscious of His nature or designation until then; (2) That He accepted it in its general spirit and purpose and in so far as it was applicable to Himself—is natural, clear, and comprehensive; and (we would say it with all deference) we do not see a satisfactory answer on any other hypothesis.

There is an account in each of the Evangelists of the events which accompanied the baptism, viz. the opening heavens and the descent of the Holy Spirit. John does not mention the divine voice, Mark and Luke represent it as speaking to Jesus Himself, and Matthew as speaking to John. Luke is very circumstantial: "It came to pass, when all the people were baptized, that Jesus also, having been baptized, and praying, the heavens were opened, and the Holy Spirit descended in a bodily form as a dove upon Him, and a voice came out of heaven, Thou art My beloved Son, in Thee I am well pleased." If we take this as the standard narrative, the less explicit accounts must be of course interpreted by it. But the balance of evidence seems to point to the position of interpreting Luke by the others. We have before seen [1] the advisability of this course. It is not for us to try to reconcile the accounts,—reconciliations are, as a rule, forced and strained,—but rather to get at, if possible, the rock of Christian tradition on which all the accounts are based. And "Luke's description of what occurred, if we had no other authority,

[1] See Note, p. 62 (in Chap. V.), and Luke iii. 7 and 10.

would suggest an objective circumstance; but since Matthew represents the whole occurrence in historical form from the standpoint of John's experience, it seems to me imperative to take Matthew and John as the true sources of information."[1]

The only points in which all the Evangelists agree are the opening heavens and the descent of the Spirit, although all the Synoptists agree in a divine voice. It is certainly a strange circumstance that the one Gospel which omits nothing that can contribute to the dignity of the Messiah should omit this. In their exposition of the voice, some writers "suppose a clap of thunder, which was imagined by those present to be a Bath Kôl, and interpreted into the words given by the first Evangelist." To this school belongs Dr. Farrar. "The Bath Kôl," says he, in his *Life of Christ*, "which to the dull, unpurged ear was but an inarticulate thunder, spake in the voice of God to the ears of John—'This is My beloved Son, in whom I am well pleased.'" But to make the Almighty resort to ventriloquism to convey a secret message,—to state that His voice was simply thunder to some, yet rumbled out an articulate sentence to others,—is not only to play fast and loose with the physical forces of the world, but to attribute to God a course of action which is unworthy because at variance with the dignity of His nature and character. Many commentators do not fairly face the subject at all, but content themselves with general and diffused remarks.

But the whole matter resolves itself into the question as to whether the appearances were subjective or objective. In endeavouring to conceive the incident as objective, there are no insignificant difficulties to be surmounted. "First," to let Strauss state them, who states them fairly, "that for the appearance of a divine Being on earth, the visible heavens must divide themselves, to allow of His descent from his accustomed seat, is an idea that can have no objective reality, but must be the entirely subjective creation of a time when the dwelling-place of Deity was imagined to be above the vault of heaven. Further, how is it

[1] Reynolds.

reconcilable with the true idea of the Holy Spirit as the divine, all-pervading power, that He should move from one place to another, like a finite being, and embody Himself in the form of a dove? Finally, that God should utter articulate tones in a national idiom, has been justly held extravagant."

If this vision were objective, would it not mark a new departure in the method by which Jehovah communed with His servants the prophets? The "voice of the Lord," or the "word of God" *came* to them and spoke in their exalted, inspired, and sensitised consciousness. It was "a conviction of surprising force and intensity"; and when it was a message for the people, it became, by thought and communion with God, at length too great and strong for retention, and burst forth in "Thus saith the Lord." Moses and all the prophets heard, believed, and obeyed these voices and uttered their messages, as the slightest examination of the records would amply show; and had they been objective, open to the eyes and ears of all and sundry, they must seriously have militated against the prophets' sacredness, their separateness of office and function as Jehovah's representatives and heralds. Micaiah said to the king of Israel: "I saw the Lord sitting on His throne, and all the host of heaven standing by him on His right hand and on His left." In like manner, Isaiah declares: "I saw the Lord sitting upon a throne, high and lifted up, and His train filled the temple. Above Him stood the seraphim," — and the prophet goes on to describe the scene in the heaven that is at once the throne-room and the temple. No one seriously considers that these visions, and others like them, existed anywhere else save in the inspired consciousness and sublime imagination of the prophets themselves. This is placed beyond doubt by the vision of Stephen at his martyrdom. Surrounded by his persecutors, he declared he saw the heavens opened, and Jesus standing on the right hand of God. Not when they saw the vision, but when they heard the testimony, they cried out, and stopped their ears, and ran upon him with one accord and stoned him. Stephen alone saw it.

We cannot but conclude, then, that the vision of John and Jesus was subjective. Reynolds concludes to the same effect: "The consciousness of the Hebrew prophet or seer, the eye and ear of the man who enjoyed such commerce as he pursued with the spiritual and unseen world, must have been opened in a way that ordinary psychological phenomena cannot explain." (This last point may be reasonably doubted). . . . "If we believe that John saw and heard these things so far as his consciousness was concerned, and said so, it will be enough to account for all the peculiarities of the Gospel narratives."

And "even in the early Church, the more enlightened Fathers adopted the opinion, that the heavenly voices spoken of in the biblical history were not external sounds, the effect of vibrations in the air, but inward impressions produced by God in the minds of those to whom He willed to impart Himself: thus, of the appearance at the baptism of Jesus, Origen and Theodore of Mopsuestia maintain that it was *a vision, and not a reality*, ὀπτασία, οὐ φύσις. 'To the simple, indeed,' says Origen, 'in their simplicity, it is a light thing to set the universe in motion, and to sever a solid mass like the heavens; but those who search more deeply into such matters' will, he thinks, refer to those higher revelations, by means of which chosen persons, even waking, and still more frequently in their dreams, are led to suppose that they perceive something with their bodily senses, while their minds only are affected: so that, consequently, the whole appearance in question should be understood, not as an external incident, but as an inward vision sent by God." [1]

Then how is it, it will be asked, that so large a consensus of opinion should have regarded, and should still regard, this vision, more especially than all others, as objective? On close inspection, the reason appears to be that objectivity is given to it by the figure employed in the description—the dove. A well-known and beautiful object is supplied for the eye of the mind to rest upon; and the "bodily shape" of Luke would suggest externality;

[1] Strauss, *Life of Jesus*.

although it need not, for the Spirit could equally well appear as a dove to the inner sight of John and Jesus as to the physical eye of the crowd. But if we interpret Luke by the other Evangelists, as we have suggested, we shall come to the conclusion that the idea is not that the Spirit appeared in the form and shape of a dove, but that the method of His descent was like that of a dove's descent "out of the heavens":—τὸ Πνεῦμα τοῦ Θεοῦ καταβαῖνον ὡσεὶ περιστερὰν (Matt.): τὸ Πνεῦμα ὡς περιστερὰν καταβαῖνον εἰς αὐτόν (Mark): τὸ Πνεῦμα καταβαῖνον ὡς περιστερὰν ἐξ οὐρανοῦ (John). Now the accounts of this vision must have been related by Jesus and John to their disciples, and it is evident they had said that the Spirit of God had descended upon Jesus in the same manner that a dove comes sweeping down from the heights of heaven to its home.

The variation in the form of the divine communication, as recorded by St. Matthew and St. Luke respectively, lends its support to our conclusion. To John the voice said, "*This is* My beloved Son"; to Jesus, "*Thou art* My beloved Son." Unless the vision had been subjective, it is not easy to see how this variation could have occurred; but on the theory that it was, the vision must, in the nature of things, have voiced itself in the different ways the Evangelists relate. We conceive that the revelation to both was instantaneous; that they united in the vision; that conviction was borne in upon the soul of each by the descending Spirit, and that Jesus stood revealed, at the same moment, both in the prophet's eyes and in his own, as "the Son of God."

And it is in accordance with this view, finally, that the psychological explanation becomes clear and simple. John had an intense conviction of the nearness of the Messiah's coming; he is the herald of a chariot that is but just behind; he has an equally intense expectation of His being revealed—He is among them; Jesus presents Himself; the moment has arrived; the conviction that "this is He" is divinely borne in upon the prophet's mind; the ecstatic vision comes, and the heavens open in his soul.

John was of the priestly order, and unconsciously has he fulfilled his priestly function of anointing and dedicating Him of whom he thought himself but the herald. Unexpectedly has he reached the highest point in the mountain-ridge of his life and ministry; suddenly his short future course lies before him. He sees at a glance the upward slope of the past. He stands "silent on a peak in Darien," looking now toward the western sea; the infinite, mysterious sea of God's redeeming purpose which lies before him, dazzling in its brightness.

"And I must decrease" is his feeling as he looks upon his own short downward slope toward it. In him had been the tentative, proclaiming voice; in Jesus the fulness, τὸ πλήρωμα, dwells: He shall baptize with the Holy Spirit and with fire.

Jesus went straightway to His temptation. He has now a new fact, the greatest of all facts, to deal with, and He withdraws into the solitude of the wilderness to let it settle into position, to estimate it at its full value, and to be tested, in view of it, by the temptation of the devil.[1]

[1] Unless the view we advocate respecting the revelation to Jesus of His nature and Messiahship for the first time at His baptism, be the correct one; that is, if Jesus knew before it that He was the "Son of God," and had therefore a pre-arranged "plan," the Temptation becomes simply an incident in the course of His life, rather than a pivot upon which His whole life turns. But this view robs the Temptation of nine-tenths of its significance and power, while the language of the evangelists in joining the Temptation to the Baptism is needlessly strong and pointed. On the position we hold, the Temptation not only retains the intense significance which in the nature of things it might be expected to possess, but the language of the evangelists receives adequate justification. After describing the Baptism, Matthew continues: "Then was Jesus led up of the Spirit into the wilderness," etc. Mark is very graphic: "And straightway the Spirit driveth Him forth into the wilderness." Luke says: "And Jesus, full of the Holy Spirit, returned from the Jordan, and was led by the Spirit into the wilderness," etc.

CHAPTER IX

"I SAW AND BARE RECORD"

WE next find John at Bethany,[1] beyond Jordan. It is after the return of Jesus from His temptation.[2] Bethany was a place probably a few miles below the exit of the river from the Lake of Tiberias, on its left bank, and over against the southern border of Galilee.

For some time now the Baptist and his work had been known to the ecclesiastical authorities, who have been waiting to see whether the movement would live, or of itself die down and become extinct. But as yet it shows no sign of being a passing, if a fervent enthusiasm ; the fire seems rather to obtain firmer

[1] "There can be little doubt that ἐν βηθανίᾳ is the true reading of John i. 28. It is the reading of a large number of MSS. and of versions. The reading βηθαβαρᾷ is avowedly a suggestion of Origen, in a passage the whole of which is given by Tischendorf and other critics."—Note in Reynolds.

[2] This seems the most probable order of the course of events. In St. John's narrative the baptism is definitely past ; it is spoken of as having taken place a while ago. It is first at Bethany (John i. 28), and shortly afterwards at Enon, near to Salim (John iii. 23), that we find John baptizing. This Salim "is no doubt the Salim of Gen. xxxiii. 18, and some seven miles north is 'Ainûn, at the head of the Wâdy Fâr'ah, which is the great highway up from the Damieh Ford for those coming from the east by the way of Peniel and Succoth. The situation was a central one, approachable also from the northward and from all Samaria, and by the central main road from the south. The assumption that the place where John baptized must have been in Judea, at least not in Samaria, is without show of proof. It should be recollected, moreover, that John's ministry was nearing its completion, and the Christ having come and entered on His ministry in Jerusalem and Judea, John might withdraw into the half alien Samaria to prepare His way there also."—Dr. Henderson's *Palestine: Its Historical Geography*, 2nd ed. p. 154. Messrs. T. & T. Clark, Edinburgh.

hold. John is again diligently preaching and baptizing. Some of the Pharisees had been attracted by the reputation of his work, and had been hotly received. Even had they been inclined to be quiet under their castigation, feeling perhaps, in secret, its truth, yet now the movement is so growing that it will not be hid. More serious notice must be taken of it. So a deputation is appointed at Jerusalem of Priests and Levites, and sent to interview him.

(*a*) To the Deputation

The "Priests and Levites" were the temple dignitaries, regarded by all, and regarding themselves, as custodians of the law and all matters religious. They were the ecclesiastics of their time, who, in their narrow conscientiousness, sent to know who the prophet really professed to be, and what his mission was. There is no need to assume that they had prejudged him, and sought only his condemnation, though the Pharisees who sent them still smarted under the castigation they had received from him in the face of the people. Probably the whole of them would be ready to welcome him, and to sanction his movement, if they could be satisfied of his credentials. But the question of ecclesiastics to one who preaches without credentials signed by them, even though he casts out devils too, is always, "By what authority doest thou these things, and who gave thee that authority?"

Armed in this coat of mail, they sought the scene of baptism, and on coming to the Baptist himself, found him in no mood to argue with them. There is a fierce reserve about him that neither invites loquacity nor bows before their office. That they should do obeisance to him has never appeared on the furthest horizon of their minds; theirs is the unquestioned right to question, and he, of course, will submissively reply. The query, "Who art thou?" is put in the tone of those who have a right to know. The first pass does not draw blood; his guard is equally quick, and is effective, "I am *not* the Christ." "What are we to make of thee, then? art thou Elijah, His forerunner, brought back from heaven, as the common report runs?" And he saith, "I am not." "Art thou the Prophet?" Shorter do his replies become,—"No."

As to this question of the deputation, the Authorised Version reads: "Art thou the Prophet?" with the marginal alternative, "Art thou a prophet?" If the question simply means the latter, John's denial is but another example of his fine humility. He is not ready to lay claim to or accept so honourable a title or office. The reference, however, seems much more specific. We take it that the article has its full definitive force—*that*, or *the*, prophet. And for two reasons. First, as against the indefinite form of the question, we can hardly avoid the conclusion that John knew himself to be a prophet of Jehovah. His training and characteristics, his meditation and communion with God, and the nature of his message, would together force such a conviction on his mind, that it is not easily conceivable how he could have answered the query with a negative. We believe that John did know himself to be "established for a prophet of Jehovah," and that he accepted the position with all its responsibilities. External evidence also lends its support to this view; "the people regarded him as a prophet." And "the people" had such a high reverence for the office, that they were not prepared to bestow it except upon those who bore strong evidence of having received the divine commission. Jesus Himself, also, in giving His estimate of His forerunner, answers His own question, "What went ye out into the wilderness to see? a prophet?" with, "Yea, I say unto you, and much more than a prophet."

The second reason carries us to a conclusion. It is that the questioners had some definite prophet in mind. The reference in their question is doubtless to the clear promise given by the great lawgiver in Deut. xviii. 15-18. "From among (the priests and Levites) the Lord thy God will raise up unto thee a Prophet from the midst of thee, of thy brethren, like unto me; unto Him ye shall hearken; ... And I will put My words in His mouth, and He shall speak unto them all that I command Him." To regard the singular number as figurative of a line of prophets in distinction to the enchanters, sorcerers, or diviners mentioned just before in the same chapter, is to force the exegesis, to make an antithesis rather than to find one; while, on the other hand, there is evidence that the Hebrew people anticipated the fulfilment of the promise in a single person.

Beyond these statements they had no information or prediction respecting him or his work,—he loomed large but vague in their expectancy. In some way he would be a specially commissioned and authoritative Prophet, standing out head and shoulders above these greatest of men; he would hold a very close relationship to the Almighty, would speak with His authority, and do for the chosen people, at some point in the future of the nation, what Moses had done at its founding.

It is not surprising to find that the prediction came to be regarded as Messianic in the Christian view; but that time was not yet. "Originally," says Wendt,[1] "it was not two great human personages, but only one, who was expected to appear in the latter days. It was either a king who should be the medium of carrying into effect the divine judgment and salvation, or a prophet, as the forerunner of Jehovah Himself, who was coming to accomplish judgment and mercy. . . . The passages (John i. 20 f., vii. 40 f., cf. Mark vi. 15, viii. 28), imply that the promised prophet was not so completely identified with the Messiah in the Jewish ideas as in the later Christian view. John Baptist's negative reply to the question whether he were the Messiah did not preclude the further question, whether he were the prophet or not. But though in their surmisings as to the significance of the Baptist and of Jesus, the Jews regarded the question as to the one or other being the Messiah as distinct from the question whether either were 'the Prophet,' it would be wrong to infer from this that both a Messiah and a Prophet were expected. The expectation of the Prophet rather stood, so to speak, in a concurrent relation to the expectation of the Messiah. Those who said, 'This is truly the Prophet,' and others who said, 'This is the Messiah' (John vii.

[1] *Teaching of Jesus*, vol. i. pp. 68, 69. T. & T. Clark.

40 f.), 'had not the same view of the character of the coming dispensation which Jesus, according to their hopes, was to introduce. But though the scribes, in the time of Jesus, were wont to combine those originally distinct ideas, we must assume that those distinct ideas lay alongside each other in various ways in the minds of the people themselves."

This was the period when these two originally distinct ideas tended to coherence and unification. In the passage, John vi. 14 f., it is related that, after the miraculous feeding of the multitudes, they said of Jesus, "This is truly the Prophet that should come into the world," and sought to make Him a king. Here the title of the coming Prophet appears as if it were equivalent to that of the Messiah. In Peter's discourse at the Beautiful Gate of the temple also, the passage which promises the Prophet was quoted, and its fulfilment claimed for Jesus (Acts iii.). Returning to the deputation,—the fact that they made a distinction in their series of questions between the Christ and "that Prophet" is clear evidence that as yet the two ideas were not conterminous.

By the short, decisive reply of the Baptist his questioners are turned adrift; are altogether at sea; they have obtained nothing but negatives. Yet they must effect a landing if possible, forbidding though the coast evidently is, and go back home with something tangible. They return and continue their catechism: "Who art thou, that we may have something definite to answer when we get back to those commissioning us,—for we are a deputation; what dost thou say concerning thyself?" And, for answer, he simply reaffirms what he had formerly told his disciples: there is nothing new in it; he evidently intends to tell them as little as possible: "I am the voice of one crying in the wilderness, as said Isaiah the prophet." Then appears the cloven foot; and, after reading the note of the Evangelist, we are prepared for it: "Why then baptizest thou, if thou art not the Christ, neither Elijah, neither the Prophet?" And again does he give for answer the substance of what he had declared to the public: "I only baptize with water, but in the midst of you standeth one whom ye know not, even He that cometh after me, the latchet of whose sandal I am not worthy to unloose." And with no more information than they brought, the deputation returned.

The last-recorded reply of John is the same he had given to the general company before, with a difference. He says that He who was to come now standeth in the midst of them. Jesus was on the ground "on the morrow," and must have been present during this controversy; He had returned from the wilderness, and was now, of course, known to John as the Christ.

The view advanced in the last chapter of the subjectivity of the heavenly vision and voice at the baptism of Jesus, receives additional support from the fact that no mention is made of it in the cross-examination to which John had been subjected; yet had the appearance and the voice been addressed to, or seen and heard by, the people at large, such a remarkable and supernatural occurrence could not but have been known to his questioners, and must have appeared, in some form or other, in their catechism.

And again, if we are at first sight surprised that there is no recognition in their questions of the baptism itself, as apart from its accessories, we must once more employ the historic imagination. The baptism of Jesus was not such an important event in the eyes of the people of His own day as it is in ours; it did not mean to them what it means to us. To us it is the moment of the manifestation of the Christ to the world, the moment when He was dedicated to and accepted His position as the Redeemer of the world; to them Jesus, even if they knew of Him at all, was simply a young man from the country, just one of the crowd, with nothing to distinguish Him from the rest.

(β) To His Own Disciples.

"On the morrow he seeth Jesus coming unto him, and saith, Behold the Lamb of God which beareth the sin of the world."

What was the content of the phrase "Lamb of God" to the

prophet's mind? The exposition given by the brilliant author of *Ecce Homo* is at least inadequate. The main part of the conception he makes out to be, not the "usages of the Jewish sacrificial system," but the following :—"When we remember that the Baptist's mind was doubtless full of imagery drawn from the Old Testament, and that the conception of a lamb of God makes the subject of one of the most striking of the Psalms, we shall perceive what he meant by this phrase. The Psalmist describes himself as one of Jehovah's flock, safe under His care, absolved from all anxieties by the sense of His protection, and gaining from this confidence of safety the leisure to enjoy without satiety all the simple pleasures which make up life,—the freshness of the meadow, the coolness of the stream. It is the most complete picture of happiness that ever was or can be drawn. It represents that state of mind for which all alike sigh, and the want of which makes life a failure to most ; it represents that *Heaven* which is everywhere if we could but enter it, and yet almost nowhere because so few of us can." It is not without great reluctance and regret that we have to put this winsome picture aside as the proffered exposition of John's descriptive phrase.

Without doubt there was a meekness in the bearing of Jesus which made the title applicable ; but the uppermost thought in John's mind is not that of quiet happiness, but that of sacrifice. This is rendered indisputable by the grammar of the text. The second part of the sentence gives the signification of the first. Had the pastured lamb been the prophet's leading thought, or even a co-ordinate and separate thought, the word "also" or an equivalent must have been employed in the second clause. But there is no such addition to specify two separate movements of thought. On the other hand, the participle ($α\mathit{ἴ}ρων$), not a finite verb, is employed, which joins the second indissolubly with the first, and interprets it. Literally the sentence reads : " Behold the Lamb of God, the one bearing the sin of the world " ("" Ἴδε ὁ ἀμνὸς τοῦ Θεοῦ, ὁ αἴρων τὴν ἁμαρτίαν τοῦ κόσμου ").

The fifty-third chapter of Isaiah was much more in John's mind than the twenty-third Psalm. As we have previously noticed, Isaiah seems to have been John's favourite prophet. And we can well understand how the fiery spirit of the Baptist should find in Isaiah's words of fire its inspiration in the wilderness. The scroll of his prophecy was often taken down from its ledge in the recluse's cave and deeply pondered.

What more natural, then, than that he should think of the Messiah as Isaiah had portrayed Him?—"led as a lamb to the slaughter, and as a sheep before her shearers is dumb. . . ." "By His knowledge shall My righteous servant justify many, for He shall bear their iniquities." "Surely He hath borne our griefs and carried our sorrows." "He was wounded for our transgressions, He was bruised for our iniquities ; the chastisement of our peace was upon Him, and with His stripes we are healed." Whatever misconceptions John's contemporaries might be under, as to the person and work of the coming Messiah,—though they had dropped the suffering part out of their idea, and enlarged and magnified and materialised, too, the reigning,—yet the Baptist knew that the "servant whom Jehovah upheld" must suffer.

And from his youth up John had been familiar with the whole round of sacrificial observances, on which the figure he employed was based. As he spoke he must have thought of the blood of the slain lamb as a sin-offering. And "there was a common tradition that the Messiah's birth would involve suffering, and that the earlier portion of His work would be the expiation of the sins of Israel."[1]

Following the lowered tone in the voice of the prophet after the baptism of Jesus, we are struck with the fact that the severer aspects of Messiah's work are lost sight of; there is now no mention of the axe laid at the root of useless trees, nor of winnowing fan and chaff burning in quenchless fire ; but the meekness and peace of His bearing, aided by the application of Isaiah's prophecies, bring up instead the picture of the patient, suffering Lamb, chosen of God to bear the world's transgression.

[1] Reynolds.

On the repetition of his testimony next day, "two of his disciples heard him speak," and "left him and followed Jesus." Without doubt John felt their going away,—they departed to the stronger; but the Baptist had understood and accepted his own tentative position; and it found both its trial and its compensation in that his own disciples were the first-fruits of his testimony to his greater successor.

(γ) "The Son of God."

"And I saw and bare record that this is the Son of God." We look at Jesus and His work through the golden haze of intervening centuries; look upon a finished work and a completed revelation. Everything about Him has been studied, estimated, and put into systems. But this rounded completeness could not possibly present itself to the minds of His contemporaries.

As Dr. Reynolds says, "We cannot attribute to the Sanhedrin or the early disciples the full significance that the phrase subsequently acquired in the minds of the Apostles or Evangelists. It became very soon the recognised formula of the faith, 'I believe that Jesus is the Son of God.' In that confession, however, we have the metaphysical and theological, as well as the national, signification of the phrase." To John, most of the facts of Christ's life were in a future he never saw, and therefore, doctrines about those facts were, in the nature of things, entirely beyond his ken.

At the risk, then, of wearying iteration, we must again ask our question—not, what does the phrase "Son of God" mean to us, after all these centuries of Christian teaching? but, what did it mean to the Baptist? what was his concept of the title?

It is quite in accordance with the idiom of Hebrew thought that anything which was abnormal or super-eminent should have attached to it the name of God; and this in reference to inanimate things and things even outside the Jewish nation. In speaking of the incomparable wealth and privilege of Tyre,—

"every precious stone was thy covering," etc.,—Ezekiel says (xxviii. 11, *et seq.*): "Thou wast in Eden, the garden of God"; . . . "and I set thee so that thou wast upon the holy mountain of God." The reference in the latter phrase is evidently not to Jerusalem, but to her own mountain, here poetically taken to illustrate the high natural and spiritual privilege of the city.[1]

The place where the Eternal revealed Himself naturally received the addition "of God." Moses led his flock to the back of the wilderness, and came to "the mountain of God, even to Horeb," where he saw the burning bush, and received the divine commission to deliver God's people. When Daniel prays for Jerusalem, he presents his "supplication before the Lord his God, for the holy mountain of his God." And the evidence that Jerusalem and its "holy hill of Zion" were especially regarded by all the Jews as "the city of God" "and the hill of God," is so abundant and so well known, that there is no need to give it here *in extenso.* But from it all we readily see how natural is that whole body of thought which considers the place "which God had chosen to place His name there"—the tabernacle or the temple—as being specially His, and which still calls church or chapel or house of prayer "the house of God."

Coming into the human sphere, and turning to the earliest records, we read that the "sons of God saw the daughters of men that they were fair." But this description "sons of God" is not here given because of any outstanding goodness or moral superiority over other men,—as a matter of fact they were much the reverse, as the record shows,—but simply because they were of larger stature and great prowess. They were *nephilim*, giants. "To the eye of the historian there loom through the obscurity of the archaic times before the flood, colossal forms, perpetrating deeds of more than human savagery and strength and daring: heroes that seemed formed in a different mould from common men."[2] It is on these physical grounds alone that this title is given them.

[1] In Ps. lxxx. 10, we read of "cedars of God."
[2] Dr. Dods on *Genesis.*

But if these would justify the title, much more would closeness of moral relationship or spiritual privilege. If we turn to Exodus (iv. 22), we read respecting the people of "God's own possession," "Thus saith the Lord, Israel is My son, My firstborn: and I have said to thee (Pharaoh), Let My son go, that he may serve Me." And in Hosea (xi. 1) we also read, "When Israel was a child, then I loved him, and called My son out of Egypt." "Son of God," "firstborn of God," are here given to the children of Israel themselves. We are not surprised, therefore, when we find these high titles given to the kings of the people. Thus in 2 Sam. (vii. 14) we have the Almighty's promise respecting David, "I will be his father, and he shall be My son."

The language and title of the second Psalm, although undoubtedly and strongly Messianic, also undoubtedly refer to David or Solomon or one of the Hebrew kings in the first instance,—most probably to David.

'Yet have I set My king
Upon My holy hill of Zion.
I will tell of the decree:
The Lord hath said unto me, Thou art My son;
This day have I begotten thee.
Ask of Me, and I will give thee the nations for thine inheritance,
And the uttermost parts of the earth for thy possession."

With this compare the language of the eighty-ninth Psalm (26, 27), also referring to David—

"He shall cry unto me, Thou art my father,
My God, and the rock of my salvation.
I will also make him My firstborn,
The highest of the kings of the earth."

But from the first, the second Psalm has been regarded as Messianic.[1] "The singer's words are too great to have all their meaning exhausted in David, or Solomon, or Ahaz, or any Jewish monarch. Or ever he is aware, the local and the temporal are swallowed up in the universal and the eternal. The king who

[1] See Dr. Perowne's *Commentary on the Psalms.*

sits on David's throne has become glorified and transfigured in the light of the promise." It was probably the language of this Psalm which at once elevated and contracted the sphere of the application of the phrase "Son of God." Certain it is that the whole nation of Jesus' day, and the disciples of the early Church, regarded the title as purely Messianic. Peter quotes it in his sermon on the day of Pentecost, and applies it to Jesus as the Christ (Acts ii. 34, 35): "For David ascended not into the heavens; but he saith himself—

> The Lord said unto my Lord, Sit Thou on My right hand,
> Till I make Thine enemies Thy footstool.

Let all the house of Israel therefore know assuredly, that God hath made Him both Lord and Christ, this Jesus whom ye crucified."

It is quoted to the same purport and with the same application in Peter's prayer, recorded in Acts iv. 25, *et seq.*; in Paul's sermon in Antioch of Pisidia, Acts xiii. 33; in Heb. i. 5, *et seq.*; in Heb. v. 5.

By the time of John and Jesus, this phrase, Son of God, had come to designate Him who stood out in Jewish thought and hope above the race, and who held such a special relation to Jehovah as the earthly Head of His people, as to justify its limitation to Him. In other words, it was one of the titles of the Messiah. *He* was especially worthy of that designation who should restore the kingdom to Israel, make the theocracy once more a living fact, and rule in Jerusalem righteously, while all the kingdoms of the earth should be subject to His sway and bring their riches to His feet.

King of the Jews, Messiah, and Son of God appear to be synonymous and interchangeable terms. That the first two are, there is no question, and examination shows that the third is so joined with them as to be evidently intended to be an exposition of them and they of it.

As we have seen, John recognised Jesus as the Messiah by this title at His baptism. And that John continued so to understand it is clearly seen from his doubting message to Jesus when in prison: "Art thou He who should come, or do we look for another?" for Jesus is not taking the expected line of action; there is no visitation of wrath, no restoration of the kingdom. For answer Jesus points to Messianic works : "The blind receive their sight, the lame walk, the lepers are cleansed, the deaf hear, the dead are raised up, and the poor have the good tidings preached to them."

The countrymen, contemporaries, and disciples of Jesus evidently understood the phrase "Son of God" as equivalent to Messiah. "One of the two that heard John speak and followed him was Andrew, Simon Peter's brother. He findeth first his own brother Simon, and saith unto him, We have found the Messiah (which is, being interpreted, Christ)," or Anointed. "He brought him to Jesus" (John i. 40). Nathanael's statement is very clear and explicit in its juxtaposition of the two; he answered Jesus, "Rabbi, Thou art the Son of God; Thou art the King of Israel" (John i. 49). "But who say ye that I am?" He asked His disciples on one occasion. "And Simon Peter answered and said, Thou art the Christ, the Son of the living God" (Matt. xvi. 15, 16). Here the second clause fills out in Peter's mind the meaning of the first, and for this penetration he received the Master's commendation. In the story of the raising of Lazarus (John xi.) Martha makes the confession: "I have believed that Thou art the Christ, the Son of God." Toward the end of his Gospel, John tells us "that these things are written" in it—referring to the content of his writing—"that ye may believe that Jesus is the Christ, the Son of God" (xx. 30, 31).

One of the subtlest parts of Jesus' temptation in the wilderness was the appeal to His newly-realised Messiahship,—the suggestions that, as He was the Son of God, He should use His new-found power to make bread of stones, to satisfy His natural hunger; His new-found special confidence in His heavenly Father, to trust Him while He cast Himself down; and, subtlest of all, that, as He was the Son of God, and there should be given to Him "all the kingdoms of the world and the glory of them, He should take a short and easy road to the realisation of the promise. Simply "bow down and worship me," said the devil,—"acknowledge me as the source of Thy authority, the one from whom Thou takest Thy commission, and they shall be Thine." The evil spirits, too, in the demoniacs, dreaded lest, as the "Son of God," He would exercise His Messianic power in casting them out and banishing them.

In the sense of Messiahship did the High Priest and the Sanhedrin understand the phrase at the trial of Jesus : " I adjure Thee by the living God, that Thou tell us whether Thou be the Christ, the Son of God." Solemnly, as putting the last, the decisive question, did he ask it, and to it Jesus answered : " Thou hast said." And that He, Jesus, the carpenter of Nazareth, the artisan who was an itinerant preacher, poorer than the foxes and the birds, whose following was among the poor, too, and the least instructed ; who had come with nothing of the pomp and blazonry of the expected king, proclaimed no crusade against the power which held them down, but had even recognised it ; who had taken no steps for the aggrandisement of His own nation and the subjugation of others ; to whom the prophet's pictures of the glorious King and kingdom were totally inapplicable ; who had done none of the expected works of Messiah ; who had opposed their party and their authority at almost every point ; that He should claim to be the hope of Israel and to fulfil it in His own person and work,—that was too much for them, and they said, and sincerely felt, " He hath spoken blasphemy."[1]

[1] Even Dr. Liddon (*Lectures on our Lord's Divinity*, 8th ed.), amid all his special pleading for the title as expressive of nature rather than of office, admits that "it is indeed probable that of our Lord's contemporaries many applied to Him the title Son of God only as an official designation of the Messiah" (pp. 246, 247). And if the above interpretation of the trial of Jesus be the right one, as we contend it is, then Jesus' condemnation was not upon the ground of divinity of person, but upon His Messianic claim. Again, respecting Peter's confession, "Thou art the Christ, the Son of the living God," Liddon says : " If St. Peter had intended only to repeat another and practically equivalent title of the Messiah, he would not have equalled the earlier confession of a Nathanael, or have surpassed the subsequent admission of a Caiaphas" (p. 11). As regards the confession of Nathanael (John i. 49), "Thou art the Son of God, Thou art King of Israel," we do not

"The primitive Christians were Jewish, alike in their ideas and hopes. Their creed was comprised in a single dogma,—'*Jesus is the Messiah.*' . . . Their preaching of the Gospel strictly follows the lines of the Messianic tradition."[1] This was the theme of Peter's preaching on the day of Pentecost. Jesus was proved to be the Christ by the resurrection of the dead. David, "foreseeing this, spake of the resurrection of the Christ, that neither was He left in Hades, nor did His flesh see corruption. This Jesus did God raise up, whereof we all are witnesses." This, also, is the single proposition of his summing up : "Let all the house of Israel know assuredly that God hath made Him both Lord and Christ, this Jesus whom ye crucified" (Acts ii.). Peter's sermon to the people who assembled, on the healing of the lame man, at the gate of the temple called Beautiful, has the same thesis (Acts iii.). It was in the name of Jesus, as the Christ, that the lame man had been restored. "The God of Abraham, and the God of Isaac, and the God of Jacob, the God of our fathers, hath glorified His servant Jesus . . . By faith in His name hath His name made this man strong. . . . Repent ye therefore, and turn again, that your sins may be blotted out, that so there may come seasons of refreshing from the presence of the Lord ;

see in what point it exceeds that of Peter. It does not seem, if anything, to equal it, for Peter emphasises God as living, and gives that title to Jesus which includes King of Israel, and much more. While as to the "admission of Caiaphas," we do not find where he made any. The reference given (Matt. xxvi. 63) shows that the high priest examined and questioned Jesus, but He admitted nothing. On the contrary, the high priest rent his garments, and charged Jesus with blasphemy. Further, Canon Liddon says (p. 11) that if we construe Peter's language thus (*i.e.* Messianically), " it is impossible to conceive why either the apostle or his confession should have been solemnly designated as the selected Rock on which the Redeemer would build His imperishable Church." It is altogether true that the content of the Messiahship was much larger in the mind of Jesus than in that of His disciples, but we hold that it was just the Messiahship of Jesus which formed the rock foundation upon which He would build His Church. We do not see how any other interpretation is possible. Dr. Liddon, so it would seem, reads back our fuller and completer doctrinal knowledge into the minds of those who, from the nature of the case, were precluded from it.

[1] Sabatier's *Apostle Paul.*

and that He may send the Christ, who hath been appointed for you, *even* Jesus. . . . Unto you first God, having raised up His servant, sent Him to bless you, in turning away every one of you from your iniquities." This, and the expectation of the Messiah's speedy return to earth to inaugurate His reign, formed the binding and unifying beliefs of the infant Church.

This—Jesus as the Messiah—is also the burden of St. Paul's *first* preaching. As soon as he recovered his sight and was baptized, he "straightway in the synagogue proclaimed Jesus, that He is the Son of God." He "confounded the Jews which dwelt at Damascus, proving that this is the Christ" (Acts ix.). He expounds the same thesis at Antioch in Pisidia. "Of this man's (David's) seed hath God, according to promise, brought unto Israel a Saviour, Jesus; when John had first preached before His coming the baptism of repentance to all the people of Israel. And as John was fulfilling his course, he said, "What suppose ye that I am? I am not He. But behold, there cometh one after me, the shoes of whose feet I am not worthy to unloose. Brethren, children of the stock of Abraham, and those among you that fear God, to us is the word of this salvation sent forth." And Paul went on to preach Jesus and the resurrection (Acts xiii.). At Thessalonica the theme is the same. Here was "a synagogue of the Jews, and Paul, as his custom was, went in unto them, and for three Sabbath days (or weeks) reasoned with them from the Scriptures, opening and alleging that it behoved the Christ to suffer, and rise again from the dead; and that this Jesus, whom, said he, I proclaim unto you, is the Christ" (Acts xvii. 2, 3).

We have travelled beyond the time of John the Baptist, and have found a uniform meaning in all the thought of that age attached to the phrase, "Son of God." Returning, then, to the Baptist, are we not bound to come to the conclusion that to him, as to all the rest of his contemporaries, this title had an ethical, theocratic, Messianic content and meaning, and that only? If John had understood it to mean absolute divinity of person and nature, as the Church now understands it, is it possible that, within a few months, he would doubt whether Jesus was the Christ? Would not that belief have settled, as on a sure and tremorless basis of confidence, every possible question and surmise? It was reserved to the future to expand it to a higher and fuller meaning. When, therefore, John pointed Him out to his disciples as "the Son of God," he simply recognised Him as the expected national Messiah, designated of Jehovah to, and now qualified for, that office.[1]

(*b*) "THE BRIDEGROOM."

Although the public work of Jesus was now definitely begun, yet the great prophet did not slacken his effort as if his work was accomplished. The next time we see him after his testimony to Jesus is at Ænon, near to Salim, where he is still baptizing. His "decrease" will be a gradual rather than a sudden one. The kingdom of heaven needs all the earnest and sincere spirits who are willing to dedicate themselves, and upon none of them will John bar the gate. The line of action which the Christ will take the prophet does not know, and in the uncertainty he will not stay his hand. Jesus Himself, however, and His disciples, have adopted the rite of John as their own, and the kingdom is large enough for the disciples of both, although the characteristics, the preaching, and bearing of the younger are cast in another and much more popular mould than those of the elder prophet.

John is still a solitary, though among the crowds; there ever hangs about him something of the gloom of the great and lonely mountains, or the inhospitable desert, to which he now and again withdraws as though going to his home. So much so, that, notwithstanding his work, the people came to the conclusion that he had a "demon,"—an indwelling spirit besides his own, that impressed upon him his fate or destiny and impelled him to it, —a natural conclusion for a life of such startling contrasts to produce in such an age.

[1] See Note B.

But Jesus took roads altogether different,—those which led Him to the haunts and companionships of men. He talked with them easily, naturally, winsomely. He caught Peter by His insight into his nature, and the bestowment of a new name. Philip answered to His call at once. The interesting conversation with Nathanael in the orchard won him to the confession, " Rabbi, thou art the Son of God, thou art King of Israel." He accepted with pleasure the invitation, and went with a smile, to the marriage feast at Cana ; visited His home for a few days ; then went up to Jerusalem and manifested His power by the cleansing of the Temple ; and then taught Nicodemus under cover of the night. In short, He did not shun, He sought, the beaten tracks of men ; He put Himself into their life, ate at their tables ; and by His personal charm, His profound insight into the Law, the expositions that brought the kingdom of God, and God Himself, within reach of the poorest and lowest if sincere, and the firm integrity of His life, He won men on every side. So strong were His social habits, so readily did He identify Himself with the people for their upraising, that the " unco guid " curled their lips at the mention of His name,—He was " gluttonous and a wine-bibber, a friend of publicans and sinners." No wonder, then, that when He began to baptize, " all men came to Him."

It was singular that two such, and so different, men should be using the same rite, singular at least to the people ; singular enough to be reported to the forerunner. If the reporters had the slightest expectation of rebellion or adverse comment on the prophet's part, they were not gratified. How sublimely— sublimely because meekly—he met the new fact ! Ever since the baptism of Jesus he had doubtless expected some such procedure on His part, and fully does he accept it. " A servant," said he, in effect, " can only go so far as he is commissioned. To be the Christ was not given me from heaven. You yourselves know that I said I was but the herald sent before Him. I am not the bridegroom, whose honour it is to marry the heavenly bride and make her his own ; I am his friend, his ' best man,' who leads him to her home. That is my office, my only office. It is not in my own position alone that I rejoice, and yet I rejoice that I have this honour ; it is in His joy I rejoice ; this, *my* joy, is now fulfilled. Then, having done my work, I shall retire : He must increase, but I must decrease." [1]

How superior he rises to all littleness ! If there is a tinge of the sadness of resignation, there is no taint of envy, in all his words and bearing. He has conquered that ambition which, as Milton says, is " the last infirmity of noble minds " ; if indeed he had ever possessed it. " He was content to be like the cheap fir, under whose shelter the young oak roots itself, and which in a little while is cut down, and gives place to the nobler tree." [2]

Such is the attitude and such the spirit of the last of the prophets ; the greatest of the Old, the courier of the New, Dispensation. Like the waning moon on the western horizon at the dawn of day, his light pales before, and at length is lost in, the glory of the rising Sun.

[1] The friend also presided as master of the ceremonies in the marriage procession and the feast. It was an important day for him, and a responsible one ; but, his work finished, he drops back out of view, leaving the bridegroom with the bride. Jesus afterwards uses this very figure to justify to John's disciples the conduct of His own. " The air of gladness which reigned around Him (Jesus) surprised them (the disciples of John). Accustomed to fasts, to persevering prayer, to a life of aspiration, they were astonished to see themselves transported suddenly into the midst of the joys attending the welcome of the Messiah " (Renan). And in surprise they ask, " Why do we and the Pharisees fast oft, but Thy disciples fast not?" And taking the former language of their own master to answer them, He said, " Can the sons of the bridechamber mourn as long as the bridegroom is with them ? but the days will come when the bridegroom shall be taken away from them, and then will they fast."

[2] A. K. H. B.

CHAPTER X

ON THE STEEP SLOPE

By the period at which our narrative has now arrived, the Baptist had become the one sensation of the country. Like a stone dropped into the placid pool of Jewish social life, from him waves of reputation have been spreading in rapidly widening circles. And the ruler, Herod Antipas, soon felt their oscillation beneath his keel.

Herod was well aware of the kind of people with whom he had to deal. He knew the inflammable material (if we may change our figure) of which the people were made, knew also that another kingdom had been their dream and hope for long generations, that this was their most sensitive and caloric spot; and that they would, at any moment and at any sacrifice, respond to the call of a religious fanatic, and rise against their rulers in the endeavour to establish it. He may wake up some morning and find he has another Maccabean revolt on his hands. The movement, if not at present dangerous, may suddenly become so.

Josephus gives this as the reason of John's arrest. He says: "Now, when (many) others came to crowd about him, for they were greatly moved (or pleased) by hearing his words, Herod, who feared lest the great influence John had over the people might put it into his power and inclination to raise a rebellion (for they seemed ready to do anything he should advise), thought it best, by putting him to death, to prevent any mischief he might cause, and not bring himself into difficulties, by sparing a man who might make him repent when it was too late. Accordingly he was sent a prisoner to Machærus . . . and was there put to death."[1]

Doubtless Josephus gives the ostensible reason, the reason that appeared on the face of the warrant; doubtless, also, it was a true one. But it was the only one of which he was cognisant, and to him it was sufficient; he sought for, and probably suspected, no other. The standpoint of the historian was that of a watcher and chronicler of political currents and events. These only does he see. He was not within even the wider circle of the Baptist's influence, much less within the inner one of personal acquaintance or discipleship, where reasons more minute, and more exact and forceful, could have been given.

The evangelists give another reason (which, however, does not shut out that of Josephus), to see the incidence and feel the force of which we must go back and wide a little in our history.

Herod Antipas not only knew the explosive nature of the people over whom he reigned, but was well enough acquainted with their history and literature to know the immense value they set upon the person and work of a prophet. They looked upon one of this high order as being specially inspired, in closest communication with Jehovah, almost himself semi-divine. And now one of that great spiritual order which all had thought a vanished race, which had formed the best and most sacred part of their nation's heritage, whose lives and works had shone luminous through the darkening years, is actually in his territory and within his reach.

Does an invitation, in the first instance, come to him from the palace? Probably so; but if it does, then without question, fear, or hesitation, the prophet accepts it. Jehovah's hand holds open another door, and he must enter. The prophet draws no line of demarcation, his message is for all, rulers and ruled alike. The demand for righteousness knows none of our social distinctions.

But while he is making his way through the valleys and along the hill-slopes toward the palace of the tetrarch,—probably at

[1] Jos. *Antiq.* xviii. 5. 2.

Tiberias, which he had rebuilt, and where he had erected a splendid palace,—with the people through whose neighbourhood he passes dogging his footsteps, watching his every movement, and gladly, yet with awe, ministering to his few and simple wants, let us see who it is into whose presence he will shortly come.

The chronicle of the Herodian family is, for by far the greater part, a chronicle of the "sensual, carnal, and devilish" order. It is not an attractive or a savoury task to study such a mass of moral decadence and defilement. But enough must be shown, even if but in outline, to place in its true significance the visit of John, and to give us the key to the tragedy that followed.

Herod Antipas, the tetrarch of Galilee, was the son of that Herod, misnamed the Great, whose character can only be summed up as a compound of unprincipled lust and unscrupulous bloodshedding. Antipas lacked the strength of will of his father, but equalled him in lack of conscience. To him, as to his father, no sanctities of home, character, or relationship were sacred if they stood in the way of his gross, degraded passion, or the schemes of his ambition.

His wife was the daughter of Aretas, king of Arabia Petræa, whose dominions, lying on the east of the Dead Sea, included the city and castle of Machærus, the latter of which he, while retaining the ownership, assigned to his daughter and her husband as one of their palaces. On one of his visits to Rome, Herod lodged with his half-brother, Herod-Philip,—not the tetrarch, as is often supposed, but the only Herod living in a private station.[1] The hospitality of his brother he repaid by intrigue with his wife,

---

[1] "Herod Philip I. (Philip, Mark vi. 17) was the son of Herod the Great and Mariamne, and must be carefully distinguished from the tetrarch Philip. He married Herodias, the sister of Agrippa I., by whom he had a daughter, Salome . . . Herod Philip II. was the son of Herod the Great and Cleopatra. He received as his own government, Batanea, Trachonitis, Auranitis, (Gaulonitis), and some parts of Jamnia, with the title tetrarch (Luke iii. 1). . . . He married Salome, daughter of Herod Philip I. and Herodias." — Smith's *Dictionary of the Bible.*

Herodias, "who was the daughter of Aristobulus their brother, and the sister of Agrippa the Great." She admitted his address, and "an agreement was made for her to change her habitation, and come to him as soon as he returned from Rome : one article of the marriage also was this, that he should divorce Aretas' daughter" (Jos.). But the faithlessness and machinations of her husband became known, by some means, to the faithful and high-spirited wife, and "she desired him to send her to Machærus, which is a place on the borders of the dominions of Aretas and Herod, without informing him of any of her intentions. Accordingly Herod sent her thither, as thinking his wife had not perceived anything : now she had sent a good while before to Machærus, which was subject to her father, and so all things necessary were made ready for her by the general of Aretas' army, and by that means she soon came to Arabia, under the conduct of the several generals, who carried her from one to another successively, and she soon came to her father, and told him of Herod's intentions." [1]

Aretas did not make known his secret purpose of revenge, but steadily prepared for war, leaving territorial matters as before. Herod therefore saw no danger from far-off Arabia, and continued to hold the castle of Machærus as his own, as the sequel shows.

And now the way was open for the guilty pair to be married, if we dare call their adulterous and incestuous union by such a high and holy name. So they live together,—Herod, whose divorced wife is still alive ; and Herodias, his sister-in-law and niece, whose husband is also still alive.

Toward their Galilean residence the stern Baptist comes, meditating many things, but calmly resolute on the one clear duty before him. No account is given us of their meeting, but we can imagine it. We see the tall form of the prophet at the palace door ; the bending sinuosity of its soft-raimented attendant ; the ushering into some silent, gorgeous room, — for the

[1] *Antiq.* Bk. xviii. 5. 1.

Herods had great taste in architecture, and loved display. We can see the tetrarch in his robes of office, as near the kingly purple as he dares to go, and assuming the "pomp and circumstance" of kings as much as may be, entering in through the parted curtains. Before him stands the respectful but unbending form of the rugged prophet of the desert, his camel's hair mantle and his long rough staff contrasting strangely with the soft luxuriousness of his new surroundings, and about him "the smell as of a field which the Lord hath blessed."

"Consider the meeting of these two men from the opposite extremes of life, of the most opposite character, and in the most opposite conditions. The one brought forth in silken luxury, the other cradled in nature's roughest couch; the one bred in the midst of plenty and pleasure and power, the other in the midst of hoary deserts and savage creatures, and fed upon locusts and wild honey, and within whose lips no luxury had ever passed; the one clothed in incorruptible truth, stripped of every ornament and grace, the other adorned with every ornament and grace of life divested of sincerity and truth." [1]

We do not know whether Herodias, like an earlier Drusilla, joined Herod, another Felix, and stood before John, another Paul; but the probability is she did. It was not the first time, nor the last, that wrong, deep and high, sat in power, while the royalty of truth and right stood before it, either as a prisoner, or in danger of becoming one.

To ordinary men the temptation is strong to modify the message in accordance with the audience. It is not a difficult matter to thunder forth in generalities of condemnation to an assembled multitude; but it is quite another matter to stand to the same guns, firing them at individuals in "thou art the man!" And the wickedness of the people is more often castigated than "wickedness in high places." Are not the edges of truth sometimes softened in the presence of wealth, or genius, or power, and is not the head sometimes bowed before "the golden image

[1] Ed. Irving.

which Nebuchadnezzar the king has set up"; or in "the house of Rimmon, when my master leaneth upon my arm"? Still greater is the requirement made on courage when the individual application is as an axe laid to the root of "the wicked in great power, spreading himself like a green bay-tree."

"It is refreshing," says Robertson of Brighton, "to look upon such a scene as this,—the highest, the very highest moment, I think, in all John's history; higher than his ascetic life. For, after all, ascetic life such as he had led before, when he fed upon locusts and wild honey, is hard only in the first resolve. When you have once made up your mind to that, it becomes a habit to live alone. To lecture the poor about religion is not hard. To speak of unworldliness to men with whom we do not associate, and who do not see *our* daily inconsistencies, *that* is not hard. To speak contemptuously of the world when we have no power of commanding its admiration, *that* is not difficult. But when God has given a man accomplishments, or powers, which would enable him to shine in society, and he can still be firm, and steady, and uncompromisingly true; when he can be as undaunted before the rich as before the poor; when rank and fashion cannot subdue him into silence; when he hates moral evil as sternly in a great man as he would in a peasant, there is truth in that man. This was the test to which the Baptist submitted."

But the seers, upon whose vision had risen eternal things, who had beheld the "Lord, sitting upon a throne, high and lifted up, whose train filled the temple"; upon whose lips the seraphim had laid the consecrating fire, and whose commission was directly of God, were not likely men to "pale their ineffectual fires" before a "man, vain man, drest in a little brief authority." Moses did not falter before Pharaoh, nor Nathan before David, nor Elijah before Ahab. Neither did Herod overawe the Baptist.

John had convinced the people of their sins; had shown that repentance meant to go and humbly "do the first works" of charity and social helpfulness; he had hurled his fierce anathemas and most scathing epithets at the "highly respectable" and smugly religious ; without fear or favour he had applied the code of divine ethics to particular cases, telling the tax-collectors to be honest, and the soldiers to be humane, truthful, and obedient. And the same principles he does not shrink from applying now. It is not on the far and general horizon that the lightnings play of "righteousness, continence, and judgment to come"; he "reproved Herod for all the evil things that he had done." And with swift directness does the final stroke descend—"It is not lawful for thee to have thy brother's wife!"

Into the free, pure air outside the prophet strode, leaving Herod to settle within himself the stirred " dregs of conscience still within him"; and Herodias to plot her deep revenge. "Therefore Herodias had an inward grudge against him," as Mark, with one of his graphic touches, says,[1] "and wished to kill him." Here is the direct and inner reason of John's arrest and imprisonment, "for the sake of Herodias, his brother Philip's wife." And it is in accordance with the fierceness and relentless hatred of Herod's paramour.

Only for a brief while does John retain his liberty. The hand of arrest is shortly laid upon him, and he is consigned to the gloomy border fortress of Machærus.[2] It would seem, from the probabilities of the case, and from the gospel narratives, which show Herod's court shortly after to be at Machærus, that Herod took John with him there as a prisoner, in order to have him near him. Away from him, John was not safe from his wife's venge-

---

[1] Ἡ δὲ Ἡρωδιὰς ἐνεῖχεν αὐτῷ, καὶ ἤθελεν αὐτὸν ἀποκτεῖναι (Mark vi. 19).

[2] The reasons given for John's imprisonment by Matthew and Mark hardly coincide. According to the former, the arrest of the Baptist arose from Herod's personal initiative, and "he would have put him to death," but that "he feared the multitude, because they counted John as a prophet." While Mark's account shows it to have been owing to the danger John was in from Herodias, who "set herself against him, and desired to kill him ; but she could not, . . . for Herod kept him safe." Matthew's account needs reconciliation, for if Herod had longed for an opportunity to put John to death, he would have seized it gladly when it presented itself at the feast ; but the record says, "the king was grieved," and with this the account of Mark also agrees.

ance. She wished to kill him, but could not; for "Herod feared John, knowing that he was a righteous man and a holy, and kept him safe."

When away from his wife, he often brought his prisoner out, and after every conversation with his faithful monitor Herod was troubled; to hear him was like bringing out his better nature into the light and air for a while. But he was too weak to decide upon the only righteous course. He put his conscience, as he did the prophet, into prison again, although "he was much perplexed, and heard him gladly." He was

"Between the full-incensed points
Of mighty opposites,"

his conscience and his passion. He found that

"Boundless intemperance
In nature is a tyranny."

Too powerful a hold had Herodias upon him. Both sacred and profane history afford many and well-known instances of men who became, similarly, slaves of tyrannous and guilty passion. The degradation of the best becomes the worst. A virtuous woman is the crowning ornament of life's temple, but a woman who has lost that which makes the charm and strength of womanhood, defiles the temple. And she may develop a power as fascinating as it is fatal. Brilliant, beautiful, and unscrupulous, with heart and moral sense repressed by main force, despite their protests, and the forces of her nature running into unnatural channels, she will develop Medusa coils, and woe to the man on whom they fasten. Cruel as the grave, they will drag him down to the deeps of sorrow, humiliation, and death.

Such a woman was Herodias; and John was to her not so much a reproof as a menace. Could the prophet bring the king over to his side, what was her position worth? And if he should send her away, where could she go? Therefore she "bore him an inward grudge"; and deeply did she plot, keenly did she watch, and heavily did she stake to "remove" him. The sleek and hungry tigress, and the man she wants to make her victim, are in their wrong places, as "in the corrupted currents of this world" they often are; the man is in the cage, the tigress outside the bars. Yet for the present she cannot "get at" him; from his wife's vengeance, "Herod kept him safe."

The Baptist's incarceration was not so strict but that he could freely see his disciples. His person and safety secured, there is no call nor desire for the rigours of close confinement. From his prison as headquarters he directs the work and journeyings of his active agents. Like Jesus after him, and Wiclif, and Wesley, John's mission was spread by itinerant preachers, and to him from time to time they made their reports, and from him sought counsel and direction.

The growing influence of Jesus, the works He did, His power with the people, and His departure, as the Gospels show, on such matters as prayer and fasting, from the method of the Baptist, must often have been the theme of perplexed conversation between the prisoner and his preachers. At last, in anxious doubt, John sent a deputation of his disciples to Jesus, to know if He to whom he had given testimony as the Messiah was indeed and of a truth the One to whom all had looked forward as the nation's deliverer.[1]

We can well understand how John, in this gloomy fortress prison, should get down-hearted. His had been a life of freedom, going on God's free earth and in God's free air where he would, but now, a prisoner, he is condemned to a life of inactivity, in the cold and dampness of a cell.

Yet this is by no means the chief reason of John's depression and pessimistic outlook. The personal element is very secondary. It is the growing doubtful question whether his life's work has not been a failure. No longer is he able to be a voice crying, "Prepare in the wilderness the way of the Lord." His soul has burned in longing for the kingdom of heaven to come, and in this prison

---

[1] See Matt. xi. 2. This verse is a side light on the accepted Messiahship of Jesus in the writer's mind: in fact, he assumes it as unquestioned: "'Ο δὲ Ἰωάνης ἀκούσας ἐν τῷ δισμωτηρίῳ τὰ ἔργα τοῦ Χριστοῦ, πέμψας διὰ τῶν μαθητῶν αὐτοῦ."

the unconcerned and heartless days and dreary nights come and go without a sign. The world rolls on as if the Lord were not mindful of His own, but had left the world's affairs to take their course. And He to whom he had looked, for whom he had been willing to take the second place, whose sandal-latchet he had felt unworthy to loose, because He was the Lord's anointed to this high office, and who at the baptism had been manifested as such, —He is not fulfilling the Messiahship as he had expected.

He had expected to hear a far louder voice than his own call from the deeps the great tide of national righteousness, which should bring to its desired haven the vanished theocracy. That tide was at its lowest ebb, and almost forgotten, but when it should come in on the flood, in the might of it they would rise and claim their land for God. The prophetic mind has always looked for judgment, it was the main part of the prophet's function to proclaim it. Doubtless the great prophet earnestly inquired of his evangelists, as they from time to time visited his gloomy prison to report their work and receive directions, whether He to whom he had borne witness were setting Himself to realise the kingdom, and whether there were any signs of an insurrectionary movement, or whispers of secret instructions from Jesus as the "head centre," the whole of which had for their purpose to cast the invader out of the land, and "restore the kingdom to Israel."

But there are no such signs or sounds; Jesus is disappointing all their hopes. His career is developing itself in unexpected ways. He refuses to be made a king. There is no axe, no fan, no quenchless fire. He preaches longsuffering, His works are not of vengeance, but of mercy. In short, neither the person of Jesus, nor His sayings and doings, nor His kingdom, were such as John expected. "What wonder, then, if the eye of the caged eagle began to film?" And can we not deeply sympathise with the man who sees the ruin of his hopes, but is powerless to prevent it; who feels like a broken instrument, cast aside and forgotten; feels that "my way is hid from the Lord, and my judgment is passed over from my God"?

At first we are surprised at the answer which Jesus returned to John, an answer which simply pointed him to the very works which had helped to raise the prophet's doubts :— "The blind receive their sight, the lame walk, the lepers are cleansed, the deaf hear, the dead are raised up, and the poor have the gospel preached unto them." That is, Jesus reaffirms the significance of these works, and asks John to find in them the true evidences of Jehovah's Messiah. And, as we have already seen, that the Messiah should do such works was part of the original concept of His character and activity.

And surely these works are such evidence. These are the works,—works of mercy and help, tidings of hope to the poorest and lowest, which have been characteristic of the world's Messiahs,—those saviours of their fellows who have had the same mind in them that was also in their great Master. It has also been the fate of such to raise doubts, and sometimes censure and opposition, in their sincerest friends and fellow-helpers. The well-known histories of Luther and of Wesley, as well as those of other reformers, afford illustrations of this. Such have always frightened their friends by going beyond the fences of precedent on to the heath, even though their purpose was to reclaim it and bring it into cultivation.

It is both significant and instructive to note the nature of the reply of such. It has never been a quotation, but always an *ipse dixit*. There has been no appeal to authority, to preconceptions of "oughtness" in the methods of their work. It has ever been the practical reply of Jesus, pointing to good works and beneficial fruit as their justification. In fact, this is the only reply that can be given. Yet it is amply sufficient, and entirely decisive. Every religious movement finds its justification, its only but its complete justification, in its rebuke of disease and suffering, its amelioration of the social environment, its offering to the sorrow-stricken "the garment of praise for the spirit of heaviness"; in its proclamation of an evangel that brings men to know that the tender mercies of God are infinite, and opens to the least and lowest the doors of an eternal hope,—a hope that is full of immortality and everlasting life.

This was the reply of Jesus to his forerunner's doubting message. For all that lay beyond it, Jesus does not enter into explanations ; He asks John to trust Him,—"Blessed is he who shall not stumble at Me." But the Baptist's was a limited vision ; in this respect, as in so many others, "he who is least in the kingdom of heaven is greater than he."

And as John listens to the reply, brought by his itinerants over hill and dale from far-off Galilee, again the old numb feeling comes back, but now with an added touch of sadness ;—"It must be right, I must trust Him : He must increase, but I must decrease." And behind those fortress walls and gates, the strong spirit of John brooded till it drooped, as the days went by, of lost liberty and of broken, vanishing hopes.

CHAPTER XI

OVER THE PRECIPICE

NOT long had Herodias to wait before "opportunity gave the leer of invitation." Herod's birthday approached. It was to be celebrated in the castle of Machærus, with all the pomp and circumstance the Herods loved.

This important border fortress stood, as Josephus tells us,[1] "on the border of Arabia, and had a prospect toward that country." "The nature of the place was very capable of affording the surest hopes of safety to those who possessed it . . . for what was walled in was itself a very rocky hill, elevated to a very great height." "It was also contrived by nature that it could not be easily ascended, for it is, as it were, ditched about with valleys on all sides, and to such a depth that the eye cannot reach their bottoms . . . for that valley which cuts it on the west extends to threescore furlongs, and did not end till it came to the Lake Asphaltitis; on the same side it was also that Machærus had the tallest top of its hill elevated above the rest." Approaching it from the river Callirhöe, travelling due south, and crossing the Wady Z'gara, with its stupendous ravine, Dr. Tristram tells us that it has precipitous cliffs eight hundred feet high on one side, and runs down by a series of steps three thousand eight hundred feet to the Dead Sea.

Herod the Great had recognised the strategic value of the mountain and castle already there; "he therefore surrounded a large space of ground with walls and towers, and built a city

[1] *Wars of the Jews*, Bk. vii. c. vi.

there, out of which city there was a way which led up to the very citadel itself on the top of the mountain ; nay, more than this, he built a wall round that top of the hill, and erected towers at the corners, of a hundred and sixty cubits high ; in the middle of which place he built a palace, after a magnificent manner, wherein were large and beautiful edifices. He also made a great many reservoirs for the reception of water, that there might be plenty of it ready for all uses, and those in the properest places that were afforded him there. Thus did he, as it were, contend with the nature of the place, that he might exceed its natural strength and security (which yet itself rendered it hard to be taken) by those fortifications which were made by the hands of men. Moreover, he put a large quantity of darts and other machines of war into it, and contrived to get everything thither that might anyway contribute to its inhabitants' security, under the longest siege possible."

As the tetrarch's birthday approached, the city of ten thousand inhabitants on the slope of the hill, as well as the castle and palace on its summit, is in increasing commotion. The invited guests begin to arrive : at first daily, then almost hourly ; the nobles, the army officers, and the most prominent government officials ; and the many-coloured cavalcades wind up the steep road to the citadel. Arriving there, they are greeted by the open-handed, pleasure-loving host, and by the smiling hostess, whose deep and secret train is laid. She

> "Looks like the innocent flower,
> But is the serpent under't."

The "convenient day" at last arrived. We do not know the free, cheerful diversions of that day, but we do know the events of the night that closed it. And the day has sped ; the night has come. The great banquet-hall, with its purple hangings and rich appointments, is lit up by a thousand golden lamps, which, suspended from the roof by silver chains, cast bright radiance upon the feast below. The cares of office are laid aside by host and guests alike; choice viands load the board; the best wine the palace boasts freely flows.

At length the feast is over; silent and quick attendants remove the broken remains, and the floor is cleared. The next item on the programme of the night's orgy is a dance. Hot with wine and meat, the passions of the host and his guests must next be inflamed. In the feasts of Eastern courts, it was usual for the indecent and suggestive dance to form a part, and the dancers were, as was to be expected, mostly of a certain class. But the guests can hardly believe their eyes when the daughter of the hostess herself enters as the dancer. We dare not attempt to describe that dance.

But she has danced, this princely maiden, descendant of the Maccabees, and now she stands before the king, with heaving breast and sparkling eyes, in all the intoxication of her innocent youth and beauty, to receive the dancer's customary gift. The infatuated king replies, "Ask what thou wilt, to the half of my kingdom, and I will give it thee, I swear it." Flushed with her success, the girl flies to her mother,[1] waiting behind the hangings of the door,—"What shall I ask? the king has promised me anything, to the half of his kingdom!" The supreme moment has come; the deep plot, carefully prepared, in which she has so boldly played her daughter, is on the verge of success. "Ask for the head of John the Baptist!" and the fierce eyes of the mother show no sign of relenting at the questioning gaze turned up to them. We long to find evidence that Salome revolted from the horrible request, but are not able,—"immediately, with haste,"

[1] According to the Authorised Version, there is a discrepancy between Matt. xiv. 8 and Mark vi. 24. The former says, "And she, being instructed beforehand by her mother"; the latter, "And she went forth and said to her mother, What shall I ask?" The Revised Version heals the breach by rendering the former, "And she, being put forward by her mother" ('Η δὲ προβιβασθεῖσα ὑπὸ τῆς μητρὸς αὐτῆς), a meaning which allows of Salome coming out of the banquet-hall, as Mark relates she did. We certainly feel relieved when we find that Salome is spared the charge, which the Authorised Version's rendering of Matthew would allow, of being a deep-scheming fury like her mother.

she went into the banquet-hall, and amid its silence said, "Forthwith give me, in a platter, the head of John the Baptist!"

The king had never dreamed of this. "He was grieved and exceedingly sorry." He sees how he has been outwitted; how, behind all, his wife's fell purpose has "stalked like a ghost." But he sees no way of escape from his oath. And he who has broken most of the laws of God, and trampled upon the sanctities of home and character, now proceeds to stand upon his honour,— "*for his oath's sake.*"

No innocent course is open to him. He had to make his choice between two evils,—to break his word, or to kill John. But, in the first place, he had promised that which was not his; and if in the intoxication of the time he thought at all, he must have known it was a promise entirely beyond his power to fulfil. Then what would the emperor say to his giving half his kingdom away to a dancer, or indeed to anybody? And, further, the head of John the Baptist did not come into the catalogue of the property of his kingdom; it formed no part of its available assets; it was not his to give. As anyone may see, this is the position Herod ought at once to have taken. But what clear thinking is possible when a man is drunk? and what firm resolution when the will is enslaved? And so, although John's

> "Virtues
> Pleaded like angels, trumpet-tongued, against
> The deep damnation of his taking off,"

the order was given, and one of the soldiers told off to execute it. One would not, for all the wealth of the Herods, have been that soldier. Roman though he was, stern, "careless of the single life," how he must have loathed his task.

We need not follow too closely behind him as he goes down the stair to where John broods in darkness and solitude, bearing up his noble heart against the circumstances that wear and the doubts that assail it. We had better perhaps remain in the hall of the feast and the dance, with the sobered revellers, whose attempts at laughter are spasmodic and feeble, whose movements are uneasy, and upon whom there has fallen an oppressive silence, for they know of the tragedy being enacted below.

The great prophet is dead!

> "Nor steel nor poison,
> Malice domestic, . . . nothing
> Can touch him further."

With the silent bitterness of deep contempt the soldier carries the head and places it upon the trencher. They hear him coming toward the hall. It is given to the dancer-princess, who carries it to her Jezebel mother. Her revenge is now complete. It is terrible! But of the two heads, the living that bends over the dead, the gleam of satisfied revenge in its eyes, the less repulsive is that upon the platter. It is even more pleasant to think of the execration of the guard-room than of the gloating of Herodias over her prey; for, soldiers though they were, and familiar with deeds of blood, they must have appreciated the noble character and the strong, pure life of the prisoner they had guarded. They certainly knew enough to know that his beheading was not so much an execution as a murder.

So sank the sun of John's life, behind sombre clouds, blood-tinged, bringing up again the old, dark mystery,—why, if the God of righteousness reigns, such lives are permitted to come to such ends. Right, in prison and beheaded: Wrong, on the throne and at the feast.

"And his disciples came, and took up his body, and buried him, and went and told Jesus."

CHAPTER XII

JESUS: AND NEMESIS

THE estimate of Jesus on His forerunner may fitly conclude our study of his life. It was spoken to the multitude who had heard the doubting message from the prison, and all of whom "counted John as a prophet." Did it strike the tender soul of Jesus that the people before Him would feel His answer to be somewhat harsh to the prophet whose circumstances bespoke their pity? For He has not answered his question, He has simply pointed out His Messianic works, and based upon them, if not a veiled reproof, at least a request that sounds like a warning,—"and blessed is he, whosoever shall find none occasion of stumbling in me." Are they coming to the conclusion that the message might have had a tenderer tone? then Jesus will remove that by showing He did not lack any sense of the greatness and value of John. He not only knew generally what was in man, therefore in the Baptist among the rest; He was his kinsman and his friend; He appreciated him more highly than they all.

"What went ye out into the wilderness to behold?" Not alone to answer them and put them down does Jesus raise this and its companion questions, but also to elevate by each answer His hearers' conception of the magnitude alike of the character and work of the Baptist. Men do not put themselves to the trouble of leaving homes and occupations and going toilsomely into the broken, barren wilderness to gaze upon a lonely bunch of reedy grass swaying to and fro, tossed about with every wind. Nor was the prophet such a feeble character that that is his fitting illustration ; in him dwelt nothing fickle nor inconstant. He was rather like one of the firm-based hills among which he walked, and which he had made his silent companions. Neither circumstances nor men had made him waver in his integrity ; the sinning ruler had met with a rebuke as strong as the sinning subject. From the straight line of truth he never deflected, nor did he temporise to gain, nor to keep it after it had come unsought, that popularity which is proverbially fickle. The " way of the Lord " he prepared was the way he trod himself,— " straight," though it led to the dungeon and to death.

Neither was it a supple courtier who aroused their attention and interest in the desert. One who studies comfort, luxury, ease ; the server of his time ; who falls in with his surroundings and asks no awkward questions ; soft-tongued to flatter, and flexible to every whim of his lord, is not likely to be found out there in the wilderness. Its bareness, coldness, hard fare, and rough life would go completely across the soft fibre of his nature and be unendurable, while its isolation would breed in him a most intolerable *ennui*. John's character corresponded with his dress, his food, his surroundings. In him the spiritual was ever first, and the flesh a poor second. The sins of the time, the felt presence of Jehovah, the nearness of the expected kingdom, shut out even the consideration of creature comfort. The perfumed ease and cushioned life, the " gorgeous apparel " and " delicate living " of kings' houses were as far as the poles asunder from his desires. The desert and the prison he could, he did, face, yet even as he faced them he had no longing for the courts of kings.

" What then ? a prophet ? yea, I say unto you, and much more than a prophet." There was no need for Jesus to emphasise the power and fruitfulness of his preaching, for " all the people, and the publicans, . . . had been baptised with the baptism of John." But it had been as though he had seen God and talked with Him, and had come for no other purpose in this world but to declare His whole counsel and commandment. The living coal from off the heavenly altar had touched his lips, consecrating and endowing him; as a lamp well lit and bright, he burned,—with all his faculties and with an earnestness which had made no reservations. Distinct from the surface-glancing lustre of platitude and social custom, he *burned*, shining so that all eyes were drawn to the brightness of his light, a light of hope that gladdened all. The effect of his preaching had been greater than that of the law and the prophets who had prophesied before him. For from his day the kingdom of heaven had been energised with new forces,—a new unit of power, which, moreover, unified. We have seen both the methods and the truth which accomplished this. Under him the slumbering instincts of God's property-right in, and lordship over, them, had been thoroughly aroused. These truths he had re-vitalised; no longer were they the dead legacy of a vanished past; they were the people's choicest and most vital inheritance.

But why "much more than a prophet"? Because he was the link of union between the two Dispensations. The deep significance of the Old he summed up in himself and carried to its highest point of development; he felt also the disquieting movements of the New. With the left hand he took hold of the departing, unwillingly relaxing his grasp; with the right he seized, though hesitatingly, the coming, Age. Yet his was the privilege of time, and of relation to the Messiah which all the rest of the prophets had necessarily lacked,—the runner before His chariot, the clamant voice, "Prepare ye the way of the Lord." "In his career it was given him to do two things,—to inaugurate a new *régime*, and also to nominate a successor far greater than himself."[1]

The more we try to study and to realise the character and work of John, the more does his figure grow upon us. We see the meaning of his training in the quiet priestly home, and of the long banishment in the wilderness; we listen to the trumpet-call for repentance and preparation for the coming King, to his demand for righteousness of life, to the calm, stern rebuke of

[1] *Ecce Homo.*

wickedness in high places; and we feel the truth of the Master's eulogium,—"Among them that are born of women there hath not arisen a greater than John the Baptist." But that part of his work which was of main importance after all was, and still is, to point to the world's Redeemer,—"Behold the Lamb of God, which beareth the sin of the world."

Under the approval and benediction of the Son of God John passes from the pages of history. But not into "the infinite azure of the past." Such a death rather contributes momentum to such a life than stops it, a momentum whose pulsations do not lessen but increase their force with the lapse of years. For the spiritual world is an inverted cone whose base is "in the heavenlies" and whose apex touches the earth; the higher we rise into it, the wider becomes the circle of the action of its forces.

The best in us is touched and vivified, coals are kindled by such fires from Jehovah's mouth. It is impossible to extinguish them. Jehoiakim may run his penknife through the record of the law and cast it into the brazier on the hearth, but the law itself is not burned, *that* remains. Herod may "kill the body" of the Baptist, but the Baptist's spirit and truth and power remain; God has taken care to add them to the spiritual treasures of His children.

It is not the comedies, but the tragedies that are charged with humanity's uplifting. The balance-wheel of the moral world is compensated. But what of those by whom the offences come? Has the soul of justice inherent in the whole of things any accounts to settle with them? Are we permitted, now and again, to see the retributive mills grinding, slowly? Do evil deeds "return to plague the inventor"? Does "even-handed justice commend the ingredients of the poisoned chalice" to the lips of the wrong-doer? Is Herod allowed to escape and to have no bands in his life or death? Let us turn to the Gospels.

One short passage in the Synoptists is a small window in an otherwise blank wall,—blank, that is, as far as the Scriptures are concerned. But a small window may afford an extensive view. The fame of Jesus, of His wonderful teaching and His "mighty works," spread in widening circles, as in the case of John before Him, and also reached and agitated Herod. "When Herod heard of the fame of Jesus, he said, It is John whom I beheaded : he is risen from the dead." To what a condition of restless conscience, ever-present foreboding, are these few words the index-finger !

To an Eastern mind his crime was the greatest of all,—he had laid sacrilegious hands upon and destroyed one of Jehovah's anointed, one upon whose head Jehovah's consecrating hand had been laid, whom Jehovah's voice had commissioned. The King's messenger he had seized and killed ! What broodings by day ! The sense of an ever-present, silent, overhanging vengeance ! "Upward he dares not look." Nor will "all great Neptune's ocean wash this blood clean from his hand." The spectre of the murdered prophet will not lie. "It haunted him, and would give him no rest. When Christ's fame arose," says Irving, "he sought to see Him that he might be satisfied it was not the Baptist. Such way had this servant of God made upon this arch-servant of the devil, that he had not only sway in life, but in death domineered over him. From his ashes he spoke to the tyrant. His blood spoke loud from the inmost dungeon of the palace into the ears of the prince ; it planted thorns in his unholy couch ; it slew his enjoyment with his mistress, and rankled like poison in his breast."

And what startings and tossings on his unholy couch in the dark, dead night !

"The affliction of those terrible dreams
. . . shake him nightly."

That one should rise from the dead presented no difficulty to the minds of Herod's contemporaries, except the Sadducees. And Herod was a Sadducee. But, as Wesley finely says, "Sadduceeism staggers when conscience wakes." And he had enough of that which doth make cowards of us all to split off the veneer of a cultured scepticism and show the grain of the real soul below.

External trouble also menaced him. Aretas would not brook the insult to his daughter. "So Aretas made this the first occasion of his enmity between him and Herod, who had also some quarrel with him about limits of their country of Gamalitis. So they raised armies on both sides and prepared for war, and sent their generals to fight instead of themselves; and when they had joined battle, all Herod's army was destroyed by the treachery of some fugitives ... Now some of the Jews thought that the destruction of Herod's army came from God, and that very justly, as a punishment of what he did against John who was called the Baptist."[1]

But Herod owed his final fall to his wife.

> "The gods are just, and of our pleasant vices
> Make instruments to plague us."

Her "vaulting ambition overleaped itself, and fell on the other side." Higher dignity still than that for which she left her "former" husband, tempted her. Closely related to ambition is envy, which cannot bear to see another prosper. Herod had a brother, Agrippa, who before-time had been a poor man, even to living on Herod's bounty, but whom Caius had raised to be "king of Philip's tetrarchy, who was now dead." Herodias reproached her husband for being contented with his position, instead of aspiring to at least as great a dignity as his brother. At length he yielded to her expostulation, and, accompanied by her, set out for Rome, to make his request of the emperor.

Agrippa, on learning their intentions and preparations, sent "presents to the emperor, and letters against Herod," in which he accused him of having been confederate with Sejanus, and of being now confederate with Artabanus, king of Parthia, in opposition to the government of Caius; "as a demonstration of

[1] *Antiq.* xviii. 5.

which he alleged that he had armour sufficient for seventy thousand men in his armoury. Caius was moved at this information, and asked Herod, when he arrived, whether what was said about the armour was true; and when he confessed that there was such armour there, for he could not deny the same, the truth of it being too notorious, Caius took that to be a sufficient proof of the accusation, that he intended to revolt. So he took from him his tetrarchy, and gave it by way of addition to Agrippa's kingdom; he also gave Herod's money to Agrippa, and by way of punishment, awarded him a perpetual banishment, and appointed Lyons, a city of Gaul, to be his place of habitation." [1]

As for Herodias, we are glad to find the relieving trait of faithfulness in the fall she had brought upon her husband. Between this Lady Macbeth of the New Testament and that of the great dramatist there is a very close analogy. It is consummate art which relieves the lurid and deepening gloom of the latter tragedy by the touch of free, sweet, innocent, and loving external nature. Macbeth's castle, though it has deep plot and dark passion within, has yet "a pleasant seat" and "nimble air," which tempt "the temple-haunting martlet" to "make his pendent bed and procreant cradle" upon its "coigns of vantage." "Where these most breed and haunt, the air is delicate."

Then the terrible plot takes hold again. But we find the parallel to this relief, in the human character that is rapidly descending to Avernus. Unsexed Lady Macbeth is, and filled from the crown to the toe full of direst cruelty; every just and tender instinct is repressed by a fierce and fiery hand; yet she cannot *quite* stop up "the access and passage to remorse," there are still "compunctious visitings of nature." Even in the very hour of Duncan's murder, heaven—the heaven of her childhood, of her quiet home, and innocent life, and peaceful surroundings —"peeped through the blanket of the dark," and held her hand.

"Had he not *resembled*
My father as he slept, I had done't."

---

[1] *Antiq.* xviii. 7.

In like manner we find a mitigating trait in Herod's wife. Bad enough, unscrupulous enough she was, as we have seen. But "when Caius was informed," says Josephus, "that Herodias was Agrippa's sister, he made her a present of what money was her own, and told her it was her brother who prevented her from being put under the same calamity with her husband." But she made this reply: "Thou indeed, O emperor! actest after a magnificent manner, and as becomest thyself, in what thou offerest me; but the kindness which I have for my husband hinders me from partaking of the favour of thy gift; for it is not just that I, who have been made a partaker in his prosperity, should forsake him in his misfortunes. Hereupon Caius was angry at her, and sent her with Herod into banishment."

If this act of nobleness cannot redeem her character for us, at least let it mitigate the severity of our censure. And as our thoughts follow her into exile, let us

"Leave her to heaven,
And to those thorns that in her bosom lodge,
To prick and sting her."

In the judgment of posterity the positions of Herod and his victim have been reversed;—"the name of the wicked shall rot," does rot; "but the righteous shall be had in everlasting remembrance." The final encomium of Jesus upon His great forerunner carries us with it completely and without reserve,—"none born of women was greater than he."

"Careless seems the great Avenger
 .   .   .   .
Truth for ever on the scaffold, Wrong for ever on the throne:
Yet that scaffold sways the future, and behind the dim unknown,
Standeth God within the shadow, keeping watch above His own."

NOTE A

ON ST. LUKE I. 5—II. 52

WE are met on the threshold of our inquiry by a remarkable fact. It is on Luke alone we depend for the narrative of the birth of John, with its attendant marvellous circumstances. Matthew, Mark, and John the Evangelist begin their notices of the Baptist with his preaching and his baptism.

The whole beginning of Luke's Gospel is, in fact, unique and striking. There is first the exordium (i. 1-4), strictly Greek in its style and character, giving the reasons why he writes the Gospel. Then follows the section (i. 5-ii. 52), which, as far as the literary organisation of the Gospel is concerned, is *sui generis*, and is purely Hebrew in its character and tone. At iii. 1, we begin on the Greek level again, so to speak, and so continue. If we were to run on from i. 5 to iii. 1, we should find it quite easy and natural, and without any sense either of literary or grammatical hiatus. The conjunction δέ would then possess its rhetorical-introductory force, in place of the resumptive force it now possesses.

At first sight, then, this section (i. 6-ii. 52) seems to have rather an external adhesiveness to Luke's Gospel than to be in fibrous and organic union with it. This impression is strengthened when we enter on it. Its vitality and movement are its own. We suddenly find ourselves standing upon another range and in another atmosphere of thought. Both are different from the range and atmosphere in any other part of the Gospel. We take a step, and lo! we are in a genuine Hebraic scene, and breathe a genuine Hebraic air. By the simple change of proper names, we could imagine ourselves reading one of the exquisite idylls of the Old Testament. Angels, visions, predictions, songs of praise, miracles, are in the air about us; divine events, that touch and move the earth, are before our eyes. These birth stories, and each of their accompaniments, are stamped with Hebrew characters.

So distinct and separate is this section, that the question at once rises as to whether it is an interpolation. It is true that Marcion (about 140 A.D.) deleted it, but then he deleted other portions as well; all, in fact, which did not fit in with his heretical teaching. His deletion does not appear to possess any critical value. Its forming an integral part of the Gospel does not seem to have been questioned. The ancients received it as such, the Church confirmed the view, the best MSS. possess it, and the critics decide for including it. No other than the orthodox conclusion as to its retention seems possible.

Then how did it come into its place here? is the next question that arises, the answer to which leads us a little back and wide of the specific question to the general one of the composition of the Gospel. In the first place, we have to correct the impressions of our historical perspective. It is difficult for us to realise that our written Gospels have not always held in the Christian Church their present position of high regard and paramount authority. Yet such is the case. The first "gospels" were oral; traditions, in the pure sense of the word. "The men who were enabled to penetrate most deeply into the mysteries of the new revelation (in Christ), and to apprehend with the most vigorous energy the change which it was destined to make in the world, seem to have placed little value upon a written witness to words and acts which still, as it were, lived among them."[1]

The whole of their religious training had been averse from writing. They already possessed, in the Scriptures of the Old Testament, a body of revelation in written form which to them was divine, complete, and final. Everything was to be decided

[1] Westcott's *Introduction to the Study of the Gospels*, ch. iii.

by an appeal to it as Jehovah's law. All that was left for them to do was interpretation. The Scriptures we now call the Old Testament were, to the Jews of this period, a majestic structure, designed by Jehovah Himself, and built and finished by prophet, poet, and priest: the plan was perfect, the execution exact, nothing needed alteration or addition. The Rabbis and scribes were the certificated guides and interpreters, whose work was to explain the meaning and purport of the whole; but the idea of expansion or alteration would have been as sacrilege.

Nor had the first preachers of the new gospel any idea of adding to the sacred books. Their simple aim was to show that Jesus was Messiah, and to support and establish it by an appeal to those writings which all held sacred and authoritative. This —Jesus is the Christ, the Messiah—was their only gospel, and the only chance of its acceptance with their countrymen was its agreement with their Scriptures. To them they uniformly and finally appealed. Let the recorded speeches and discourses of the apostles be read, and this position will at once be proved and illustrated. Theirs was a "ministry of the word." It did not need to be committed to writing, not only because tradition was strongly against writing ("Commit nothing to writing" was one of the rabbinical maxims), but also because all they had to do was to show that the facts of Jesus of Nazareth's life, works, death, and resurrection were all foreshadowed in the Messianic prophecies, and that, conversely, His life satisfactorily fitted them all. There was the end.

Further, the apostolic Church was instinct with the vitalising idea of the speedy return of Jesus. "The Lord is at hand" is a constantly recurring, warning note. And as He would soon be here again to "usher in the new time of the 'age to come,' the claims of the present possessed an urgency which threw the idea of a literary provision for the future into the shade. Who would record the apostolic recollections for the sake of a posterity that would never see the light? And who would devote to such unprofitable labour the hours and the strength which might yet avail to rescue some lost souls from the doom that must otherwise overtake them?"[1]

It is not difficult to conceive the causes which must, in the nature of things, have necessitated the composition of the Gospels. The lives of the first preachers of the new gospel were those of itinerating Evangelists. In their eager endeavour to go through the cities of Judah before the Son of Man came, and to reach as far as might be the outlying world prior to that final event, their stay in each place in which they preached was necessarily brief, determined by the success of the work, or the importance of the place, or both. It was almost impossible that the few converts to the new faith, mainly of the poorer classes, could absorb and memorise, *verbatim et literatim*, the oral gospel they had heard and believed. And as the preacher on his part, when about to pass on, would naturally want to leave some more permanent memorial than his spoken words for the establishment and edification of his converts, so would they on theirs desire "some solid ground to rest upon."

A further strong need for written records is found in the variable nature of tradition itself. Its inevitable tendency is to expand, to receive new interpretations and new additions. So wide is human speech, so different the mental idiosyncrasy of each narrator from every other, that, if the elementary statement may be pardoned, it is impossible, while tradition is so fluid, to make it rigid and exact. For the sake, then, of the substance itself of the faith once delivered to the saints, it would become ultimately necessary to reduce it to writing. Even then the records will, must, bear evidences of those variations it received before it was put into permanent form.

Another reason is found in the extension of the privileges of the gospel to the Gentiles. On accepting it, these were introduced to an altogether new world of ideas. The Old Testament Scriptures were to them an unknown land. The truths and hopes which had sustained the Jewish body politic through good

[1] Carpenter's *The First Three Gospels*, 2nd ed., p. 63.

and evil report, through success and reversal, was a new aliment to the Gentile convert. It was not indigenous to their soil. For their instruction as well as edification, the written record must have soon become essential.

By no means the least of these reasons was the delay in "the coming of the Lord." There is no question, as indicated above, that throughout the entire Christian Church in the apostolic age, the expectation of the return of Christ in the clouds of heaven was supreme. But all things "continued as they were from the beginning." Members and officials,—the "eye-witnesses," became old and began to die off. The "reaper whose name is Death" cut down some of the apostolic twelve. Therefore a strong need arose for the conservation of the gospel traditions, so that they might be handed on intact to another generation.

Thus, from the itinerating habits of the first ministers, the difficulty of maintaining the gospel message in its purity, the necessities of the Gentile Churches, and the invasion of death during the delay of Christ's coming, it became imperative that the gospel-content should be reduced to the permanence of writing. Notes and memoranda of the facts, incidents, and miracles of Christ's life, of His sayings and discourses, would naturally be made, and left with the infant Churches for their edification when they came together for fellowship.

"It is certain from the testimony of St. Luke that various narratives of the whole or of parts of the apostolic tradition were current." That these were, as Dr. Westcott says, "unauthoritative or partial documents" may be granted, but, as he also says, "at the same time they may have exercised a considerable influence upon the mass of Christians, preserving among them the general form and substance of tradition."[1] Again, to quote the same authority, "parts of the tradition may have been committed to writing from time to time; many, as St. Luke says, may have attempted to arrange the whole in a continuous narrative, but still it remained essentially a tradition in the first age, and as

[1] *Introd.* pp. 205, 206.

such found its authoritative expression in our Gospels." Meyer holds the belief that these partial narratives may have existed in great numbers.[1] Dr. Ewald holds that "reminiscences of the teaching of individual men, and documents of a partial nature which were not originally designed to be regarded as anything else than partial, were the chief sources at the command of the first three Evangelists."[2]

It is now generally conceded that both the first and the third Evangelist made use of the Gospel of St. Mark. The evidence for this is extensive and readily accessible. But many scholars hold the view that, in addition to this common source, they had another document,—the "Logia." And the question is whether they derived their additional matter from this, or from the scattered and fragmentary accounts of which mention has been made. For reasons which need hardly here be discussed (are they not written by Dr. Stanton?), it seems probable that the belief in the influence of the "Logia," supposing it to exist, will have to undergo considerable modification. "We may say that the theory that both St. Matthew and St. Luke used the 'Logia' is open to many grave objections, and that it seems at all events impossible to suppose that they both used it to anything like the extent ordinarily assumed."

Finding myself in such agreement with Dr. Stanton on the composition of St. Luke's Gospel, I may perhaps give the summary of the case in his words. "There is, as I have said, strong reason to believe that St. Luke made use of the Gospel according to St. Mark. The latter probably wrote soon after St. Peter's death, say about A.D. 65; St. Luke's work may be placed soon after A.D. 70. He felt that he possessed much additional information which deserved to be recorded, and which, no less than his predecessor's narrative, was derived from 'eye-witnesses of the word.' A considerable portion of this additional matter is peculiar to St. Luke's Gospel, and there can be absolutely no

---

[1] *Commentary on Luke*, p. 261.
[2] As summarised by Dr. Stanton, *Expositor*, February 1893.

reason to suppose that it is not the fruit of his own collection of material. The third Gospel contains, however, a certain number of passages which are almost word for word the same as passages in the first Gospel, while for the most part the context and setting in these very instances are quite dissimilar in the two Gospels. The most natural account in these cases seems to be that there must ultimately here be documentary links between the two, but that the written accounts in question passed into the two Gospels by different courses. They had been obtained by St. Luke in a fragmentary form independently, and without the knowledge of the manner in which they were arranged by St. Matthew."

Returning now to the section under consideration (Luke i. 6–ii. 52), I believe that, from its special and singular character, we have here one of those partial and fragmentary narratives which St. Luke found in documentary form, and which he adopted in the compilation of his Gospel. Possibly, probably, he "worked over" it, and made it his own. For the religion of this literary man, the companion of St. Paul, was hampered by no modern doubts respecting miracles or supernatural occurrences and appearances; while its Hebrew form and setting, instead of raising any suspicion as to its authenticity, would be to him a further evidence of it.

To enter upon the section itself in detail would lead us wide of our purpose, and would, moreover, raise the whole question of the supernatural, for which volumes rather than a note would be required. Great names could be put on parade on both sides. But even if we adhered to the sceptical regiment, we should hold the interpretation of its first fact as given in the first chapter of this work, that Zacharias and Elisabeth were "advanced in their days," that is, as to the hope of offspring.

NOTE B. "SON OF GOD."

Though the conclusion has been arrived at that to the Baptist the phrase "Son of God" had a purely Messianic meaning, yet it would be unsatisfactory to leave the whole of this important subject there, seeing that the future held for it such a remarkable development. It is desirable briefly to indicate its doctrinal expansion, at least to the limits of the New Testament.

It is very evident that there is a great difference between the Christology of John the Baptist and John the Evangelist, and between that of the Baptist and that of St. Paul. St. John's Gospel was written to apply to Jesus the higher elements, indeed the highest, of the Messianic concept, and to interpret His discourses, His acts and controversies, from this high standpoint. It is granted, on all hands perhaps, that, rightly or wrongly, this Gospel contains statements about Jesus and reported statements from Jesus which imply, not only the ordinary ideas of the Messiah which, as we have seen, are current in the Synoptists, but a high metaphysical relationship with God which involves, if not actual paternity, a specially close spiritual community of being.

With this high note the Gospel itself opens : " In the beginning was the Word, and the Word was with God, and the Word was God," etc. This is very different from the material and human opening of the former Gospels. But it is well known that, long anterior to the time of Christ, the wisdom of God had been strongly personified in the Hebrew writings. Consider the striking passage, Prov. viii., which is all concerned with the personification of wisdom, a personification which (vers. 22-31) is stated to have been pre-existent to all creation—

> " The Lord possessed me in the beginning of His way,
> Before His works of old.
> I was set up from everlasting, from the beginning,
> Or ever the earth was.
> When there were no depths, I was brought forth,
> When there were no fountains abounding with water.
> Before the mountains were settled,
> Before the hills was I brought forth, etc.

In the whole of this magnificent passage, wisdom is personified as present with God in every step and act of creation, and as taking a delight in all.

Now, is it not almost inevitable that from conceptions like these there should be developed, or through them there should be revealed, the doctrine of a being at once distinct from, and yet one with God? Certain it is that John's Gospel recognises and teaches this, unless we are to understand all through that he describes simply an *idealistic* relationship of Jesus to the Father. "He was in the world, and the world was made by Him, and the world knew Him not." "The Word became flesh, and dwelt among us." "No man hath seen God at any time; the only begotten Son, which is in the bosom of the Father, He hath declared *Him*" (ch. i.). According to this Gospel, also, Jesus Himself claims this pre-existence. In His conversation with Nicodemus, Jesus says, "No man hath ascended into heaven, but He that descended out of heaven, *even* the Son of man." "God sent His Son into the world" "that the world should be saved through Him" (ch. iii.). When Jesus claimed to work miracles by the power of "My Father," "the Jews sought the more to kill Him, because He not only brake the Sabbath, but also called God His own Father, making Himself equal with God" (ch. v.). This high strain runs through the discourse which follows, in the same chapter. He is "the true bread which came down out of heaven." And when this statement mystified, not only the Jews, but His own disciples, He said to the latter, "What then if ye should behold the Son of man ascending where He was before?" (ch. vi.). That the Jews regarded these claims as Messianic is seen from the next chapter, where the people say, "Is not this He whom they seek to kill? . . . Can it be that our rulers indeed know that this is the Christ?" Their only difficulty was that they knew whence Jesus came, but no man knew whence the Christ was to come,—there was no difficulty in understanding the import of His work and claims.

In the next chapter we have Jesus' long controversy with the Pharisees as to His relationship to the Father, in which He again makes the claim to "come forth" and "come from" God, and at the end of which He states, "Before Abraham was, I am." And through all the Gospel, never does Jesus abdicate or modify this claim. It is maintained through His exposition of Himself as the Good Shepherd, through the discourse in the upper room, through His last high-priestly prayer.

There is no doubt that these claims and statements were Messianic: the question is, were they *only* Messianic? did they mean that the thought and purpose of God became an actuality—"were made flesh"—in Jesus, and that *this* was the $\pi\lambda\eta\rho\omega\mu\alpha$ which dwelt in Him? or did they mean a distinct claim to actual personal filiality of nature?

Let us turn briefly to St. Paul. According to him, the Christ was the Almighty's agent in the leading of the children of Israel through the wilderness, and in their sustentation, for "they drank of a spiritual rock that followed them; and the rock was Christ" (1 Cor. x. 4, 9). But Christ existed before the creation, was the agent of it, in fact (see Prov. viii. before quoted). "In Him were all things created, in the heavens and upon the earth, things visible and things invisible, whether thrones, or dominions, or principalities, or powers; all things have been created through Him, and unto Him; and He is before all things, and in Him all things consist (hold together)" (Col. i. 16, 17; comp. Eph. iii. 9 and Heb. i. 2). According to Col. i. 15, He is "the image of the invisible God, the first born of all creation." (As also 2 Cor. iv. 4; Phil. ii. 6.) "It was the pleasure of the Father that in Him should all the fulness dwell" (Col. i. 19). "In Him dwelleth all the fulness of the Godhead bodily" (Col. ii. 9).

All of these St. Paul, of course, applies to Jesus as the Christ. Again, the question for us is—Is this high teaching simply the more exalted part of the Messianic idea, or does St. Paul here and all through his writings teach that Jesus partook of the nature of God as a human son partakes of the nature of his human father?

Office, or nature, that is the choice. The Church has chosen and advocated the latter view. The development of the doctrine proceeded, until at length the title "Son of God" had come to mean "God of God, Light of light, very God of very God, begotten, not made, being of one substance with the Father,"—*i.e.* the entire and complete divinity of Jesus' nature and person. Whereon another great alternative rises,—Does this dogma represent the completeness of this section of the "all truth" into which the Spirit was to lead His Church? or is it that the more exact and mathematical Western mind exalted a poetic and spiritualised idea and phrase into the position, and gave it the authority, of scientific literality? These high and much disputed though most important questions cannot be discussed within the limits of a note.

Returning to St. John and St. Paul, however, we can see at a glance that they have advanced very far beyond the standpoint of John the Baptist, whose conception was, as has been stated, that the title "Son of God" was purely Messianic. In the possession of truth and privilege, "the least in the kingdom of heaven is," as Jesus said, "greater than he."

www.ingramcontent.com/pod-product-compliance
Lightning Source LLC
Chambersburg PA
CBHW030336170426
43202CB00010B/1141